Slyde in the right direction

Slyde in the right direction

Chrissie B. J. Sandison

The Shetland Times Ltd.
2008

First published by The Shetland Times Ltd., 2008.

ISBN 978-1-904746-31-7

Printed and published by
The Shetland Times Ltd.,
Gremista, Lerwick, Shetland,
ZE1 0PX, Scotland.

Contents

Contents (continued)

Contents (continued)

Dedicated to the memory of those
who shared my childhood at Slyde.

Introduction

MY mother, Chrissie Sandison, regularly contributed descriptions of her early life to *Shetland Life* magazine, starting with 'The Unseen Stores' in issue number 169, until issue 245. These were some of the significant influences and events of the first thirty years of her life. She has kept a diary for many years, so maybe one day the next sixty years can also be recorded.

For far too long the family thought "it wid be fine ta hae aa yun pittin tagidder in a book." Firstly, permission to do this was obtained from *Shetland Life*'s first editor, James R. Nicolson. Then Chrissie's grandson, Robert, word processed all the articles and sent copies to the family. It then became obvious that to turn these articles into a book was not as straightforward as simply printing them out, so nothing happened for quite some time.

Eventually I took the decision to begin the task. Spread over many months, it grew into a mammoth endeavour to remove duplication, provide extra explanation and add new information. Answers to my questions were always wide ranging and often more, equally detailed, anecdotes were told. I rarely came away with just the answer to the question asked; many of the chapters do stray on to other subjects but they were too interesting to leave out – and this is what you get when listening to my mother. I'm grateful to Laureen Johnson who gave valuable advice, including that I should "keep Chrissie's voice" so the sidetracking is part of that.

Genealogy has always been one of my mother's interests – it seemed to me as if it was the only subject ever discussed at mealtimes when I was a child. She spent many hours poring over records when Bertie Deyell was the local registrar, and often visited the Shetland Archives. As a result, she compiled quite a number of family trees, including a sizeable tome detailing many of Da Taits who radiated out from East Burrafirth. Visitors from various parts of the world have often turned up at her door looking for information, and she has exchanged letters with them and many others over the years. I have included some family trees to help those interested in sorting out who's who in the various chapters.

Everywhere my mother travelled she needed to study maps of the area; she can still accurately describe places visited many years ago. I have included some maps which are rough guides to the areas she has mentioned – any errors are mine. Again, I thought it might be useful for readers to have an idea of the area covered in these recollections.

Unfortunately, my mother's failing eyesight now makes reading nigh on impossible so she has trusted me to put the book together, with help from other family members. She has been introduced to Shetland Library's Talking Newspaper service so now gets *The Shetland Times, Shetland Life* and *The New Shetlander* on tape which she really appreciates. Sadly, this service is currently unable to provide a selection of locally written works on tape. She has volunteered that the royalties from her book sales should go to help establish this worthwhile service.

Hazel Tindall

Section 1

A Little Family History

1

Evictions from Kergord

MY parents were Thomas Anderson and Ann Jane Garrick. My Anderson ancestors were actually Weisdale folk; my grandfather, Robbie Anderson, was a son of John Anderson and Johanna Jacobson. My grandmother, Margaret (known as Mergat), was a daughter of Christie and Merran Nicolson of Quienster. Apparently she had gone to Upper Kergord as a servant to an Inkster family. Mr Inkster came originally from Burra and had been at the gold digging in Australia. He had a property at Kergord. So that was how my grandparents met in the early 1860s.

Great-grandparents

Both Robbie and Mergat were born in 1841; they married at Twatt Kirk in November 1862. I assume Mergat would have been married from her parents' home at Quienster and, if so, would have made a journey by sea to get to Aith from where she walked over the hill and down to the kirk.

Robbie had an aunt (Baabie) from Kergord, married to a man named Robbie Dalziel, who lived in a house at Da Voehead, Aith. I assume Robbie may have hoofed it there across the hill from Kergord on his wedding eve. No doubt he would have had his bottle of Faeroe brandy in his pocket! One can only guess! Maybe there could have been a primitive stag party with his cousins. Robbie, being an Anderson, wouldn't have wanted to miss out! He was not quite twenty-one years of age, but had been several seasons at the Faeroe fishing.

The marriage took place in dull, dark November, so they would have had to make an early start. For all I know Mergat maybe had arranged a half-way house too – just in case! All is a closed book; so I better proceed with what I know to be true.

Eviction in 1869

My paternal grandparents, Robbie and Mergat Anderson, and their household, were evicted from Upper Kergord during the clearances. Many a story has been told. Some get dramatised and twisted with every telling. In 1869 (at the time they were evicted) Robbie and Mergat had two children – Mary and Johnnie. Also in their household was my grandfather's mother Johanna, his teenage brothers Jeemie and Johnnie, and two younger sisters – Baabie, aged about twelve, and Meggie, who was about ten. I very much regret I didn't take my opportunity of getting first-hand information from my grand-aunt Meggie – more about her later.

As can be imagined, they all lived together in very cramped quarters, but that was what everyone was doing in those days. United they stood; divided, they knew they would fall.

From Kergord to East Burrafirth

The route my grandfather's household took when they had to leave Upper Kergord involved a steepish, steady incline up along the south side of Scallafield, until they reached Da Muckle Scord (sometimes called Setter Scord). On reaching Da Butter Stane they entered the parish of Aithsting. From here it was downhill mostly; down past the Loch o' Lunklet to cross the burn upstream from the waterfall of Ramnahol.

I think quite a few trips were made before their animals and fodder had been transported on their backs. Auntie Meggie had her nephew Johnnie in a kishie; at that time he was almost four years of age and could remember the journey quite well when he was a very old man.

The grown-ups had heavier burdens. My grandmother, who was pregnant at the time, had her burden of sheaves too. On the uphill parts my grandfather took her burden on top of his own while she carried some lighter item. I am not certain, but I think each of those families to be evicted was given 28 days grace in which to find somewhere to go and get themselves moved.

I asked Meggie how it was that they knew about a croft soon to become vacant in East Burrafirth. She told me that men from Upper Kergord were in the habit of going across the hill and down to East Burrafirth armed with docken kishies to where there was a sillock yard – a low-walled enclosure, built on the sand almost at the head of the narrow voe, in which sillocks and flukes got trapped when the tide began to ebb. After scooping up those small fishes the kishies were covered and left to drip before the men set off back to Kergord. Maybe the Kergord men would have got a drink of milk or blaand to help wash down the oatmeal brönnie which they always carried in their pockets to keep hunger at bay. Those were very hard times when folk were poor.

That was how they came to be well acquainted with the locals and that proved to be how my grandfather found out the Aest Gaet (East Gate) croft was soon to become vacant. They moved there in March 1869 and my father, Tammie Anderson, was born there in July of that same year.

They tried to get a seed crop at Aest Gaet but it proved heavy going as the faely daeks surrounding the croft had got pretty run down. I can remember Auntie Meggie telling how they each had to take their turn at keeping an eye on those hill daeks, night and day, so as to prevent sheep invading their crofts. Grandfather, like so many others, was a fisherman so couldn't have been at home much, except for short spells. I do not know for sure exactly how long they stayed at Aest Gaet but I was told my father was the only child born there, so I assume they moved to Slyde in the early 1870s, where six more sons were born.

The previous tenant of the Aest Gaet croft had been a widow, Jeannie Caddle (Calder). Her husband, Jeemie Tait, had died in 1861. She and her two teenage daughters found it an uphill job to keep the croft going so they left and went to Innersand where her folk still lived. Betty Tait, one of Jeannie Caddles' daughters, eventually became my grandmother on my mother's side. She married Jeemie Garrick.

Move to Slyde

An Abernethy family had been living at Slyde but their family had all moved away, so when the parents died in the early 1870s Slyde became a vacant croft. Slyde had a much older name of Ongwall – which in my opinion is much the better name. We used to wonder about this old name and why it got changed to Slyde. Maybe that only came about after the Crofters Act was passed in 1886.

In the earlier census returns, I found East Burrafirth in the parish of Aithsting. The first couple of houses (near the voe head) were referred to as the Punds o' Burrafirth; further up I came upon four or five houses under the heading 'Hamlet of East Burrafirth' which included Wasthoose. Next came three crofts (of which Ongwall was the middle one) all under the heading 'Lea of Burrafirth'. The very last croft on that paper was Quienster, that being the croft on the north boundary of Aithsting where it joins up with South Delting. So I wonder whether it would only have been after 1886 that all those crofts were given individual names. How Slyde came to be named remains a mystery but the croft is a very steep area of land – perhaps one of those fellows from the Crofter's Commission had lost his footing on the steep hillside and started to slide ower da banks! We will never know.

However, we eventually discovered the place name Ongwall in Jakob Jakobsen's book *The Place Names of Shetland*, in the parish of Aithsting. The definition is given as 'the place of the narrow strait'. Very appropriate too, for quite a deep narrow straight does separate Da Skerry o' Slyde from the north-west corner of the croft. Who knows? Perhaps those bold Vikings of long ago did indeed sail a longship through da Soond o' da Skerry at high tide!

I imagine my grandmother would have been delighted to get nearer her own people at Quienster and away from those too-close neighbours whom she felt were breathing down her neck. The move to Slyde would have had its compensations. There they had plenty of space outside – not at all congested together as they must have been at Upper Kergord. Just off the shore there was any amount of fish waiting to be caught. The house had good shelter from all easterly erts of wind. Hellifield gave good shelter but when the wind blew west or north-west it could make itself felt.

A long, low house, with three rooms on a stretch, at that time Slyde had a thatched roof. In those far back days it was crammed with people. They behaved as many large families did; always someone was up during the night while the others slept. Outside work was often done by the light of the moon. Sometimes an older woman would have her sleep early on in a winter's evening then give up her bed to someone else, while she got on with carding wool and spinning on her wheel.

Babies were all born at home and people died there too. My great-grandmother was a howdie (midwife) so I imagine she had many a sleepless night. There were few doctors and no district nurses in this area before 1920. It was common in my young days for someone to come knocking on a window in the middle of the night seeking help – someone was very ill, or someone had died. Help was never refused. No one knew when his or her turn might come to require help. That was how they helped each other.

2

Paternal Grandparents

Grandfather – Robbie Anderson (1841-1919)

I have no memory of my grandfather. He died in February 1919, six months before our mother died in August. Apparently his memory deteriorated during his latter years so someone always had to keep an eye on him. He would set off north along the Lea Banks not knowing where he was going. One of my older brothers kept a little way behind and eventually persuaded him to come back home. He was seventy-seven when he died.

Grandmother – Margaret Anderson (1841-1924)

Long ago, when a family consisted mainly of sons, as one by one they decided to get married it was common-place for more than one daughter-in-law to move into the home of her parents-in-law. And so it happened at Slyde. At one time there were three lots of grandchildren there. When I was young I could never understand how it was that lots of folk in Aith could never 'redd oot da Slyde folk'. It was little wonder, I daresay, for our household would have seemed a mixed-up bunch to those who weren't connected by family ties and never came to discover 'wha wis wha'! Though, mind you, in those pre-war days there were quite a lot of houses which had two or three families under the same roof. It was a way of life vastly different from today.

I don't know for sure, but was told by my brother Robbie that our grandmother (who may well have been the one who ruled the roost!) had a big say in which daughter-in-law stayed and which one had better go! Our mother was favoured – she was a hard worker and she, having been the eldest of a large family, knew how to keep her end up. She also could turn a blind eye and a deaf ear to things which tended to annoy or irritate. A trip up the hill for a kishie of peats or other outside work to be done on the croft gave each some personal space.

Memories of my grandmother are vivid enough. I was six when she died at Slyde, rather suddenly, of influenza, just after her 83rd birthday, in February 1924. I remember her as an auld body at the side of the stove, often reading. She had four elder brothers so that way had had an opportunity to learn to read and write.

She was a peaceable woman apparently, and is the only woman I ever knew who sniffed snuff! She had a tiny snuff box. I remember one time she'd run out of snuff (you who whiff a fag perhaps understand how she felt!). No snuff to sniff caused a feeling of stress, though that word hadn't been invented in the early 1920s. Anyway, on that particular occasion help was at hand, in the shape of Christie Tait from da Punds who had come on a visit. He took from his pocket a twist of tobacco, cut off a few thin slices and rubbed it down between the palms of his hands, after which he transferred it to a lid of the stove. Next he got a teaspoon and pressed it down and stirred it round in an attempt to pulverise the tobacco into a fine powder before getting it transferred to grandmother's snuff box.

I can also remember being allowed to take a tiny pinch of snuff between my thumb and forefinger and, giving a good hard sniff, transferring it up my nose. Oh gaad! What a horrid swein sensation, and a nasty smell too. It brought tears to my eyes. Can you imagine it? Letting a peerie lass aged five sniff that villainous stuff. One wonders when exactly grandmother would have got into such a habit. Maybe it did help to ease a headache or act as a tranquilliser. Like smoking, it became a habit.

Grandmother, I have been told, always gave special advice to newlywed couples: "Let not the sun go down upon your wrath." They may not, at that time, have been acquainted with the word sorry but there were other gestures to convey the message that all was forgiven. Very good advice!

But I have many pleasant memories of my grandmother. She always sat in a chair alongside the stove, usually knitting and often singing in a low voice to herself. She would sit and rock a cradle with her foot – 'nuggin da cradle' it was called. Most houses had two cradles in those days, one smaller one for an infant and another bigger one for an older child to sleep in – a fine cosy 'beddibaa'. I remember one time grandmother kept on nuggin an empty cradle after the child had been lifted out by his mother – so engrossed was she in her reading she had not noticed that the cradle had become lighter.

There was a biggish, flat block of wood, which had 'come wi da sea', which served as her footstool. Sitting there at her feet I first learned to cast a loop (knit). First of all it would have been gertins (garters). Next I progressed to knitting a cradle-belt, which had to be quite some length as it was tied across a cradle in zig-zag fashion to prevent a child from being rocked overboard in the process of lulling them off to sleep!

On Sunday evenings she got out her hymn book and she and I would sing together many of her favourite hymns. I have a vivid memory of sitting on her footstool singing hymns on a sunshiny evening when I'd have been about five or six years old. She had a deep faith in a spiritual life after death and always the last two hymns we sang were "There's a land that is fairer than day" and "There is a happy land".

I'll never forget one lovely, sunny evening her saying, "It'll no be lang noo till I'll be goin away tae da Happy Land." She seemed so sure in her own mind that all would be well. It so happened that she passed away rather suddenly, only a few months later. When my sister Maggie told me that grandmother had died, I asked Auntie Ellen whether grandmother could indeed be away to her happy land. I received an affirmative reply so I accepted it as the way things had to be. I have accepted death news with the same calmness ever since.

Auntie Meggie

Auntie Meggie (1858-1938) – grandfather's youngest sister

I very much regret failing to ask my Auntie Meggie much more about the days of her childhood at Upper Kergord, Weisdale. I once had a splendid opportunity when she had become an old woman, only able to sit at the ben room fire at St Clair Cottage, Scalloway, always knitting away on her sock.

Circa 1936: in the garden at St Clair Cottage, Scalloway. From left: Edith Johnson (Voe), Brucie Tait (Hoit, East Burrafirth), Baabie Nicolson (nee Leask), Margaret Anderson (Auntie Meggie) and a district nurse. At the front is Baabie's son, John.

At the time she and I had our chat about old times I was only a teenager and, like all teenagers, I daresay, I was trying to see ahead, while Meggie spent a lot of time looking back – just as we all do now the sun is getting west! She was eighty years of age when she passed away.

Her father, Johnnie Anderson, died when Meggie was exactly one year old. Meggie's mother was Johanna (Hanna) Jacobson. There were four sons and two daughters in that family, and there could have perhaps been more who didn't survive because I discovered quite an age gap between my grandfather, who was the eldest son, and his two youngest brothers. Meggie herself was a peerie body while her sister Baabie was a big woman, so they were referred to as Muckle Baabie and Peerie Meggie.

Meggie the carer

Meggie's youngest brother was about four years her senior. His name was Davie and he was apparently Meggie's favourite. Her young life was saddened when he died of tuberculosis, only a lad of thirteen. She had been his nurse; his bed was of heather covered by a blanket on the floor in a corner near the fire. I forgot to ask whether it had been a fire in the middle of the floor or at the gable end. While the older members of the family were outside doing the croft work, Meggie was responsible for keeping watch over an infant in a cradle and her brother in the corner. The infant, her nephew Johnnie, had been born prematurely, so needed extra attention. Quite an uptak for a girl aged about nine!

She recalled one day she had been sent across to Setter, Weisdale, with some messages. The woman in the house was sitting near the fire on a stool, kneading oatmeal dough in preparation for baking brönnies on a braand-iron. She broke off a bit of raw leaven and gave it to Meggie who, although she was feeling pretty hungry, felt she must keep most of it for her sick brother. So she kept rolling the dough between her hands, only 'nippin aff a peerie bit noo an' dan' for herself.

They were all in a sorry state in Upper Kergord at this time. Every house (or more likely they were hovels) was overcrowded and sometimes when crops failed they were near starvation.

Davie died before the family was evicted in 1869. He was buried in the old kirkyard down at Soond in Weisdale. Meggie had a wish to be buried near to where he had been laid to rest, but by the time she passed on that section of the old kirkyard had been closed, so Meggie is buried in Aith.

In 1885, when living at Slyde, Meggie sat with my grandmother's sister, Mary Ann Hunter (nee Nicolson) at Quienster, as she died of TB, leaving three motherless children. Already in that household were another five motherless children. When the men were fishing the children were supervised by their elderly grandmother who managed to get the tatties on to boil. As she wasn't strong enough to undertake the heavy task of lifting the pot off the fire, and pouring the water off, Meggie walked to Quienster each day to help her out.

Later it was rumoured that Mary Ann's brother, Tammie, had poisoned her. He was most upset by this and arrangements were made to have her body exhumed. Meggie was with her sister-in-law (my grandmother) and niece when they were called to formally identify the body from the clothes. I don't know where this would have taken place. She told me that a surgeon was present and the deceased's stomach was removed to look for signs of poison, but all that was found was a piece of a clove.

Ale drinkings

Meggie could remember about what was termed ale-drinkings, which took place among the houses of Upper Kergord after the men folk returned from the Faeroe fishing in September, each one in possession of a pig o' brandy. As was usual when too much strong drink was flowing freely, men tended to get argumentative and more than once she remembered there would be a show of fisticuffs – just to let everybody know who was the stronger man! When things looked like getting out of hand Meggie's grandmother, Beenie Duncan, who like myself was a peerie body but unlike me had a sharp tongue in her mouth, put that to good use in quelling the boisterous merry-making. Sometimes she managed to hide a keg to be used at some future occasion!

Meggie's education

Meggie Anderson learned to read, and to write a letter too, although her opportunities were few. Only when John Johnson (John o' da Holm) came to Slyde, mainly to teach the boys, did she ever have the chance – and a poor one at that – for during these so called lessons Meggie always had an infant in her arms. But I suppose she would have picked up all that was going from her niece and her eight nephews who came along after they settled at Slyde.

Howdie

Each small community had to be self-sufficient to cope with any emergency, and they all did that well. Meggie herself saw many changes during her lifetime; she attended many births and deaths, for in her young days there were not many trained midwives, nor undertakers, but those who gained some knowledge helped when needed, unpaid.

Meggie was a howdie (midwife). She told me that when her mother, Hanna, became past middle-age she took Meggie along as a trainee howdie. Whenever there was a birth or a death at Slyde, Auntie Meggie always seemed to be there. When my grandmother died, everyone at Slyde was suffering from flu so when she arrived at the house (by then she was living in Scalloway) she diluted and drank Condy's (potassium permanganate) to kill off the flu germs. Condy's was a mild disinfectant which was available as either liquid or crystals.

A doctor was only called upon in dire straits as nobody could afford to pay a doctor's fee. When Mother Nature failed to bring about a natural birth and other complications arose it was only then that somebody was sent on foot or by boat to get the doctor.

Dr Bowie lived at Parkhall, near Bixter, and it sometimes happened that he would be away in some other district delivering another baby. He had all of Sandsting as well as Aithsting to look after and often he was called to Weisdale too. So it isn't a surprise to learn of still births. That was all accepted as being God's will.

Baby care

I asked Auntie Meggie what they used for hippins (nappies) all those years ago when everybody had to fall back on whatever nature provided. She said that in late summer older children, along with an adult, would collect lucky-minnies-oo (bog cotton) and sphagnum moss which grows in profusion in certain damp places. This stuff was stored in buggies.

A buggie was the skin of a sheep which had been 'buggie-flayed' after the sheep had been killed. The skin got a going over with lime and water (on the inside); this caused the wool to slip off quite easily. Next, I suppose it was salted and rolled up for a few days, then thoroughly washed and stretched over a large rock. It ended up something like a bucket bag. I remember buggies being used for holding raw wool and rowers ready for spinning. Those buggies would have lasted for years.

These bits of cotton and moss were used on a baby's bum and tied into place with some old pieces of cloth. When a baby was changed – always in its mother's lap – the soiled material was tossed into the back of an open fire (always nature's scavenger). After cleaning up, the small bum got a going over with goose-grease; fresh minnies-oo was laid on and a clean piece of cloth wrapped on to keep it in place – hopefully. There surely would have been soap and water used, and a towel. But long, long ago maybe soap and towels were scarce too.

They apparently had some sort of dusting powder named Fuller's Earth. Heaven knows what that lot consisted of, but in my dictionary the definition is given as a highly absorbent clay used in talcum power. But I don't remember those items being used. Terry nappies began to be produced in the early 1900s and Johnson's baby powder too. In Meggie Anderson's day there were no barrier creams, and no baby wipes. Even so, many mothers just could not afford to buy nappies and a bar of toilet soap; maybe not even a tin of baby powder to give things an agreeable smell!

I heard tell of a certain woman who had a novel way of doing things. She kept an eye on a number of grandsons while their mother was outside doing the hard croft work. Her method of cleaning up a mucky bum was to use a hard clod of peat! Then a liberal dose of goose-grease was applied – I bet none of those peerie fellows ever suffered from nappy rash!

I can remember whenever a duck or hen was killed at Slyde the wedge of fat found inside the bird was never thrown away, but rolled up in brown paper to be used for various purposes. My father used it for greasing his heels before pulling on his socks and boots before setting off to walk across the hill to attend a meeting at the Methodist Chapel in Gonfirth. That wad of fat was also used as dubbin on leather boots or the axle of a wheelbarrow. No doubt it would have become rancid but I imagine when the smell got too high another duck or hen would have been 'taen aff'! Various people kept geese, so there would never have been any scarcity of natural lubricants.

There were no playpens or cribs. It seems Auntie Meggie was chief babyminder to all her nephews. Sometimes, a big wooden tub was used to keep a toddler away from the open fire – there was no such thing as a fire guard. An ageing grandparent (or maybe a great-grandparent) always sitting near the fire would have managed to keep an eye and a hand on peerie inquisitive bairns.

So many recollections have been lost concerning those days when four generations often lived together – as nature meant them to do. A far cry from today. Sometimes, I wonder whether the time may yet come when a baby's nappy will be changed by pressing a button on a computer! Or maybe someone will push the wrong button so that disaster strikes our phoney existence, leaving everything in chaos. I hope not. It likely won't be in my time, but one can't help wondering.

Foster mother

Well, I better get back to some more concerning Meggie. Around 1884, my grandmother had produced her seventh son. He was born in April and named Christie (read more about him in the Clousta chapter). In December of that same year, a baby girl was born in a peerie house locally known as Da Star (quite near another peerie house known as Da Moon), in the South Voxter area in Gonfirth, South Delting. This baby's mother, the wife of Tammie Leask, died not long after the infant was born, leaving two motherless children.

When my grandmother Mergat heard this sad news she went to Da Star to see what she could do to help. Tammie Leask was distraught wondering what to do for the best, so he asked my grandmother if she could take the infant for a while until he found his feet again. The older child, a boy named Ollie, was apparently taken to some of his father's family at Voxter. Tammie's parents had both died when he was just a child so, poor man, he hadn't all that many to turn to. So it happened that Baabie (as the infant was named) was fostered at Slyde.

Auntie Meggie said to me, "Whin I saw Mergat comin' by da but window kerryin a bairn in a hap, I kent wha wid be da wan to look efter it!" And so it came to pass. The infant snuggled up in Meggie's bosom. There was no wet nurse available and Slyde was quite some distance away from neighbours, so Baabie had to be bottle fed on cow's milk. During the long, dark winter nights Meggie managed to keep a peerie bottle of milk warm in the bed between her and the baby. The milk would have been milked from one of the cows just before bedtime.

Of course, there were no rubber teats for a bottle in those days, but a piece of quill from a duck's wing served as an instrument to transfer the milk from bottle to baby. A bit of clean cloth was wrapped around the neck of the bottle and around the quill so as to make it more agreeable to an infant's mouth. But she would have soon learned to drink from a cup or saucer. Sometimes oatmeal was steeped in water overnight and the thickened water was boiled next day and fed to an infant from a spoon.

Anyway, Baabie was a strong infant and she thrived and grew to be a great asset to my grandparents' household. She filled the place of a younger sister to my grandmother's host of young sons, the youngest of which was born in 1887 and named Joseph. When I appeared on the scene in 1917 I was given the honour of being named after Christie, Baabie and Joseph – a proper jaw-breaker! Surely they had a premonition that I was going to be da skoor-da-buggy (the last of their family)! As was usual, babies always had to have names belonging to the family. Not so, nowadays.

1900: Baabie Nicolson (nee Leask), who was fostered at Slyde after her mother died at childbirth.

Circa 1930: Baabie with her son, John Nicolson.

Scalloway

When Meggie was middle-aged – maybe after her mother died around 1899 – she went as a servant to Berry Farm at Scalloway. She didn't speak much about that period of her life. I expect she looked after the cattle and may well have done kitchen work too, but I don't know.

Later Meggie was dairymaid at Adam Jamieson's in Scalloway – he was a merchant and a farmer whose home was St Clair Cottage. He asked Meggie if she knew of anyone who could come as a housekeeper and cook. Meggie's foster child, Baabie, had spent quite some years at service in Broughty Ferry and Edinburgh so was persuaded to fill the post. I don't know when that took place because Auntie Meggie and Baabie were together at Scalloway all my minding. When Adam Jamieson died, they were given the chance to buy the house which they paid by instalments. Baabie married Geordie Nicolson in 1925. At that time the cows were kept in a park opposite the Scord quarry and Geordie's job was to deliver the milk. They had one son, John, who used to come to Slyde for holidays once he got old enough.

One of my vivid memories of St Clair Cottage dates from about 1923, when Auntie Ellen took me to Scalloway for a week or two in December of that year. I recall attending a watchnight service in the Methodist Chapel to welcome another New Year. More vivid still is my first encounter with a modern bathroom. I was indeed really scared that I might get swallowed down the throat of the toilet! And the big bath too felt a bit scary – all that water and a bath with high sides. I feel sure (in thinking back) that I never entered that room by myself. It was all so different from what I was used to at Slyde.

Another thing I remember her saying was, "Weel, I lookit eftir Baabie whan she wis peerie, an noo sho's lookin efter me." So that's how it was. That's how nature means it to be. She had a peaceful old age, her memory recalling times from her youth, and she had no fears of being sent to 'da poor hoose', as places like Brevick Hospital used to be called. Such was life in the raw.

Peerie Meggie, who possessed a big heart which she shared with many, had a retentive memory and when she died she left many good memories to all those who knew her. There are many who don't know she ever existed and that is why I have decided to pass on a very important piece of history.

4

A Second Family of Andersons Evicted

Jeemie Anderson's family – my great-grand-uncle Jeemie

As I go on writing these memories from long ago, I find it quite impossible to pen it all without getting side-tracked on to something else. So at this stage let me refer to another Anderson family, evicted from Upper Kergord some years after my grandfather's household. This was James Anderson, an uncle to my grandfather. They came to Aithsness. One of his sons, Tammie Anderson, was the man who first set up a shop in Aith.

Jeemie Anderson apparently had a lease on his Upper Kergord croft, which meant that David Black, proprietor, couldn't evict him until some other suitable place could be found for him to be transferred to. I only assume that some sort of arrangement was made between Black and Gifford of Busta, who at that time was landlord of what is now known as the Vementry estate. There could of course have been other factors involved which I know nothing about.

Crofters had no security of tenure – that only came about when the Crofters Act was passed in 1886. Most landlords saw more profit in the rearing of sheep, so crofters were evicted at the drop of a hat!

From the Census taken in 1871 I found Jeemie Anderson and his household were still in Upper Kergord, but it may well have been in that year they moved. The names of those evicted are in Appendix 2.

Finding a new place to live

I have been told that Jeemie's youngest sister, Betty Anderson, walked from Kergord across the hill to Da Voehead in Aith, where one of their older sisters lived (Baabie was married to Robbie Dalziel). From there Betty walked round the west side of Aith Voe until she reached Aithsness. She decided there and then that Aithsness was the place they wanted – a good fertile croft with shelter from most erts of wind, and a good outrun. Never mind that the house and croft were already occupied.

So they had the task of transporting all their household goods, mostly on their backs, across the hill to East Burrafirth, where it all had to be loaded into a boat and rowed across Aith Voe to the Mark noost in the Bight o' Braewick There the boat had to be unloaded and their gear carried up to the homestead of Aithsness. The cattle would have been moved on the hoof across the hill, but I don't know about the sheep, whether they too would have been driven across the hill and around the voe or whether Black, the landlord, may have bought them. Somehow, I think their sheep were moved to Aithsness too.

Domino eviction

Two Nicolson families who were tenants at Aithsness had to get out to let those Andersons in. That was how things were in the middle of the 19th century.

From the 1871 census I found a list of Nicolsons at Aithsness: Andrew Nicolson (68), his wife Mary (not certain of her age as the writing was indistinct), son John (32), Margaret (29), Sarah (20), Thomas (11) and Mitchell (9). I am not certain about the relationships. Mary may have been Andrew's second wife. I do not know where Andrew Nicolson and his family managed to get a roof over their heads – Uyeasound near Vementry, perhaps, but that is only a guess!

The other family listed at Aithsness were Barbara Nicolson (nee Johnson), aged 59, her son Andrew (20), daughter Mary (33), another daughter Joan (25), with her husband Thomas Dalziel (33), and a baby, Robina Dalziel, aged four months. I have been told that after having to leave Aithsness, Baabie Nicolson and her family were taken in at the Quilpunds. They were there for only a very short time until they got a croft at Selivoe.

As we might try to envisage what it must have been like to be evicted from a home and separated from friends, it is as nothing in comparison to what continues to happen in various parts of the world today. Robbie Burns wrote: "Man's inhumanity to man makes countless thousands mourn." Never more so than in today's overcrowded, so-called civilised world, when it seems that man's primitive instincts still have the upper hand.

It has been said that one old woman living in the vicinity at that time prophesied that a third generation of Andersons would never live in Aithsness: whether she possessed second sight or not I do not know, but her premonition proved true.

5

Boating Tragedy, 1904

ALTHOUGH this happened before I was born, it was still fresh in the memories of the older Slyde folk, whose relatives were involved, and was still spoken about when I was young.

Edmund Fraser

William Edmund Fraser, BA, born around 1859, was son of Patrick Fraser, an Edinburgh advocate. He came to Shetland around 1892. I have been told he had a drink problem so his father sent him north hoping, perhaps, that there might be less alcohol available and a country way of life might straighten him out! I do not know for sure. I am only writing what was told to me some years ago.

He came first to Railsbrough in South Nesting. He met Beenie Anderson from Aithsness and they married in 1901. Beenie, apparently, was able to keep him on the straight and narrow by allowing him his ration of whisky and no more, but sad to say their time together was not destined to be very long.

Edmund Fraser was a man with money at his back. Sometime towards the end of the 19th century he purchased, from Gifford of Busta, the Isle of Vementry and all the land on the west side of Aith Voe, south as far as Houster and right around the head of the voe as far as Scarvataing on the east side, and also the croft of Quienster.

By 1900, Adam Dickson and his family were occupying the croft at Uyeasound, just across from the Isle of Vementry. Round about the turn of the century Edmund Fraser had a new house built there and he and his wife moved in as soon as it was finished.

Edmund Fraser had an interest to improve things and had four cottar houses built at the head of Aith Voe – Burnside, Lochside, Valleyfield and Navy Cottage. He also instigated the very first regatta ever held at Aith, in 1903. A boating club committee was set up around 1902. Fraser himself, I assume, was commodore and John Anderson, his brother-in-law, was secretary. I do not know the names of those on the committee, nor do I have the date of the 1903 regatta, but in 1904 it was advertised in *The Shetland Times* to be held on 20th October, to give those men who had been at the fishing during the summer a chance to compete. No report of the 1904 regatta appears as the secretary, John Anderson, lost his life in a boating accident the very next day.

The day of the accident

The day after the regatta, 21st October, 1904, Edmund Fraser (45), his brother-in-law John Anderson (33), along with a young servant lad named Tammie Fraser (16) (a son of Mitchell Fraser and his first wife Helen Garrick, Uphoose), and a spaniel, set out in a dipping-lug sailing boat to fetch rams from the Cow Head Holms that lie off the eastern point of the Isle of Vementry, where those sheep had been put to graze over the summer months.

The wind was squally from the south-west. The distance from the noost and around the point was about two miles – out of sight of the house. By twelve o'clock they had not returned and Edmund's wife, Beenie, became anxious about them. She went down and spoke to Mitchell Nicolson (the shepherd and crofter) who, along with Laura Robertson, had seen the spaniel all wet, though at first both had assumed she had been swimming at the noost (which was her wont to do). The shepherd hadn't been aware that the three men had gone to take the rams ashore.

Mitchell Nicolson and Laura Robertson then took a small boat and pulled out till they came in sight of the holm and, seeing the sheep grazing undisturbed, they realised that the boat had never reached there. They then pulled around the holm, and when they came to the south-west side they saw a taft, an oar, and two pieces of flooring which had landed on the shore, also two caps, all indicating that a disaster had taken place. They went back with the sad news, and a message was at once dispatched to Tammie Anderson, merchant, Gudataing, brother of John Anderson and brother-in-law to

Edmund Fraser. Search parties were on the spot all that day until darkness fell but nothing further was found.

Finding the remains

Next morning, a water glass was procured and a search was made where it was thought the boat had gone down and ultimately the boat was seen on the bottom. Shortly afterwards the bodies of John Anderson and the young lad, Tammie Anderson, were found and a buoy was placed to mark the spot. The search for Edmund Fraser's body continued till it was found a short distance from the boat but nearer the island. He had been a strong swimmer and it was supposed that he had been attempting to swim to the shore and he had succumbed. It is believed that the accident must have happened within a quarter of an hour of the boat leaving the noost at Uyeasound.

All three bodies were interred in the cemetery at Aith on Wednesday, 25th October. A feeling of shock and disbelief pervaded the whole district. Beenie Anderson did not long survive her husband. She died at Vementry in March 1906, aged around 40.

It's a wonder there weren't more fatal boating accidents. I well remember Auntie Ellen's anxiety the day she kept watch on a sail boat carrying a coffin and mourners from Quienster to Aith – it was quite windy and she couldn't understand why they hadn't arranged to carry it to the Muckle Knowe where Ertie Moffat's truck could have met them – but that was quite a long walk uphill over rough ground.

Mother's Side of the Family

James Garrick (1847-1925) and Elizabeth Tait (1849-1919)

My maternal grandmother, Elizabeth, died a month after my mother, so I have no memory of her.

Jeemie and Betty brought up their family at the Baak, Sandsound, but by the time I remember seeing my grandfather he was living at a house called Da Coarner, which was near Berfield, also in Sandsound. This house had no croft and he lived there with his unmarried daughter, Baabie (Barbara) – her death certificate gave cause of death as nephritis and heart trouble.

My grandfather had a sailboat which he used to fetch goods from Scalloway to sell in his shop in Sandsound. I'm not sure if it was down at Da Store – wherever it was there was no easy route up the very steep hillside to the houses at Baak and Berfield.

My maternal grandparents: Betty Garrick (nee Tait) and Jeemie Garrick who lived most of their married lives at Baak, Sandsound. I guess this photo was taken about 1895, after their children had been born.

I recall my brother Robbie speaking about taking his new bride to meet the Garrick family soon after he married, when my cousin Jeemie was still an infant, the son of unmarried Auntie Mimie, our mother's youngest sister. Soon afterwards, Robbie set off to sea and met up with mother's brother, Uncle Robbie, who was flytin about Johnnie Mouat getting Mimie pregnant, but it wasn't very long before Uncle Robbie found himself in the same position with Johnnie Mouat's sister, except that they got married before the baby arrived. In those days the only birth control was abstinence, and some seemed to believe that pregnancy happened only if the Lord willed it.

Section 2

Slyde and the People Who Lived There

7

Slyde

OUR house at Slyde had two storeys, with a felt covered roof; it was fairly long but not quite 12 feet wide. I can remember one winter there were eleven of us there all together. Until 1937, when I was almost twenty years of age, we had no road to the house. Peats, for heating and cooking, had to be carried from quite some way up the hill.

The croft at Slyde was a hard-working place. It required a strong workforce to keep everything in good going order. Each member of our household had his or her jobs to do. We were all aware that there was a need for everyone to pull their weight when a heavy job had to be done – "tae keep a ruif ower wir heads". Many hands make light work so we each had quite a lot of spare time. All in all, I can honestly say that our kind of life in those days was happy enough.

In 1951, the Slyde house was fixed up in the hope that one of the young folk would make it their home with a new husband or wife. At that time a permit was needed to buy wood but the permit wasn't sufficient to buy all the wood they needed. By then the wooden-roofed house at Quienster was vacant so it was arranged that the Quienster roof was dismantled, carried down to the shore, loaded onto a boat, sailed to the Nort Ayre at Slyde and carried up to the house for the roof to be finished. There was enough wood left over to build a house for storing hay.

Our old home has been vacant since 1981, although one of my grand-nephews keeps it in good condition. He and his wife work the croft and stay there a few weeks each summer.

1924: outside Slyde. Left to right: Liza, Faider, the author, Mimie, Auntie Ellen, Davie, John Robert and dog, Ertie Moffat (Gerts). I think the photo was taken by Andy Moffat who was one of Liza's boyfriends.

Treasure from the sea

A fairly deep channel separates Da Skerry o' Slyde from the mainland. During the spring tides there appeared a forest of waar blades jutting out of the water and in voar, after a storm, quite a brook of waar tangles built up on the Nort Ayre. An ever-watchful eye was kept for this windfall (or more a tide fall)! Everyone in our house who could carry a kishie was pressed into service to help carry the long tangles and slippery waar blades up the face o' da banks and on to one of the rigs. Waar was a splendid fertiliser, being rich in potash and other minerals.

My father had what he termed a kishie-man which was used as a helper when working alone at this job on the beach. When he (or anyone else) decided to rake together whatever the tide had brought ashore he always used a kishie-man. It was a sort of cross-legged wooden frame with a wooden shelf on top and also a backboard to keep a kishie upright. When a kishie was maybe more than half full, it was lifted on to the kishie-man and filled up by hand, till it was heaped up, often with tangles hanging over the top edge of the kishie. Down there at our Nort Ayre one got a strong smell of the open seashore at ebb tide.

I wonder whether anyone of a younger generation ever bothers to gather seaweed from beaches more accessible than the Ayre at Slyde, where any brooks of waar which come ashore will certainly get washed away again on the next rising tide. Nothing was allowed to be washed away all those years ago when we were a household of able-bodied folk and well trained to know that time and tide waited for no man. All other chores were left so we could make a joint effort on the beach.

Shopping

Goods bought from Aith shop came by sea so had to be carried on backs up a zig-zag pathway in the face of a low cliff, then up a steep gaet alongside the yard daek. Many a time I humped a 70lb (30kg) half boll of flour up that brae and straight upstairs to where barrels of flour and oatmeal were kept. More about shopping comes later.

Food

Most months there was always any amount of fish in Aith Voe. Many an hour I spent along with my father at the handline. Those were fish; straight off the hook, we even took a bucket of salt water up to the house which was brought to boil in a fair sized pot, in went the fish whose tails curled up with freshness!

We had a lot of hens, so were never short of fresh eggs, besides two or three milking kye. A pig was usually reared for the table – the hams put into pickle then hung up and dried in the but end. The taste of a slice or two of home-cured bacon had a taste of its own! Ducks also produced eggs in the voar and I remember my eldest brothers going egg hunting among the gulls' and dunters' nests. Sometimes more than one pail full of eggs was found in the porch in the morning. A second bucket of cold water was used to discover which were fresh eggs, and which might be sitten. The fresh eggs sank to the bottom of the bucket while those unfit for us to boil and eat were used with milk to feed young calves.

Vegetables were also grown. Usually 12 kishies of tattie seed were set – the seed came from our own crops but whenever a change of tattie seed was wanted (or to try a different variety) we swapped with friends in Muckle Roe or Wethersta. The tattie crop was stored in a tattie hol – a hole was dug, filled with the crop, covered in pones and topped with möld. Kale and neeps were grown to feed animals and humans. The kale runt (stalk) was split and fed to the cattle, along with the outer blades. The hearts were cut and fed to the lambs. Neeps were also grown and fed to sheep, cattle and humans. A few carrots were grown, for human consumption.

Food and toys found in the sand

East Burrafirth Voe is very shallow and at spring tides ebbs out quite a long way, so that Meena's Burn is the only stretch of water. If the tide was out and a need arose to get across from the Hametoon, the skyiff (skiff) had to be dragged across the smooth sandy bottom, which felt good under bare feet. While the tide was out it made a splendid playground for the children who soon learned how quickly the tide could flow back in over the sand. There they could find cockles and mussels besides spoots and smisslens.

June 1930: Slyde house in the background. Back left to right: the author, Auntie Ellen, Liza with Jean on her knee, Mary Ann Tait (Upper Pund), George. Front: John Robert, Lion the dog and Maggie. The females of the house were all wearing mourning black.

I can remember how all those were taken and cooked and later the empty shells served as playthings. Many a limpet became a goose in our childish imagination, whelks were hens and the white whelks (dog whelks) were our ducks. Yoag shells became our cows. Those with big barnacles were our milking cows – even though it took a stretch of the imagination to fix a cow's udder on her back! When we decided it was time for a cow to calve all one had to do was lift up the big yoag shell and there was a very small one underneath! All so very simple! Of course, our childish play was just imitating whatever the adults were up to. We were happy in our small world of make-believe. Living at an isolated place like Slyde, my nephew John Robert and I had no fears that other children might sneak in and destroy our miniature crofts.

Music

When I was a young child we had a phonograph in our house with quite a number of those cylindrical records, which were very brittle so had to be handled with care. Those records were mostly of hymns. I was very taken with the music and the catchy tunes – "Sing them over again to me", "Wonderful words of life", and quite a few of those old Sankey hymns.

An old phonograph would fetch quite a price in today's antique market, but somehow I feel sure that the one we had would have been thrown over the White Craig (a big rock at the seashore) after we got a gramophone! Before the days of the essy kert rubbish was thrown in the sea if it couldn't burn. It was common practice to exchange records when I was a teenager. A lot of so-called hill-billy songs, the words and tunes of which often come to the surface of memory.

Recycling

In my youth nothing was ever wasted or thrown away if it could be re-used. In the late 1930s my brothers made use of an old boat which they cut in half width-ways. One half was hauled up near to the house and used for storing cured peats – referred to as 'da paet boat'. The other half had tarred boards fixed to the cut ends to make a flootchie – a square ended skyiff.

They used another old boat, turned upside down and rested on a low wall built of stones, to make a roof for a washhouse they'd built adjacent to the spoot which gave a good supply of water. Benches were made for two zinc baths, and there was a drain for pouring out the dirty water. A small peat fire warmed the water and the clothes were put to steep (soak) overnight. Next day this bath of soaked clothes was brought to the boil then washed by rubbing the articles energetically on a washboard. We had no wringer, but that was not unusual, so usually two people did the wringing, each with an end which they twisted in opposite directions. The second bath was used for rinsing the clean laundry. Clothes of course weren't washed as often, mostly everything was worn for at least two weeks before it got a wash, including underwear, but it was much more substantial than the flimsy items popular nowadays!

There were no disposable sanitary protection items so home-made squares were made from old sheets and pillowcases. Long tapes were sewn on opposite corners for tying round the waist. The soiled squares were kept between the mattress and bed springs till washday when they were soaked in salt and water, then boiled. It was splendid when the J. D. Williams mail order catalogue started to sell disposable sanitary towels – those of course were recycled as fuel for the ever-burning fire.

I remember my mother-in-law telling me that in her young days she remembered sometimes finding bars of Sunlight soap here and there at the side of the Lerwick-Hillswick road. This was surely one of the first forms of advertising.

June 1936: Jean Anderson. The Slyde wash house is on the skyline – wash house was demolished in 1946.

In one house I remember seeing a whelp being picked off the floor and rubbed round the inside of a used frying pan till the pan was fairly clean. This harmed neither pup nor pan, and gave the pup's mum a bit of a feed as she licked it clean! I don't know if the pan was washed afterwards. But I don't remember that happening in Slyde!

8
Mother

Ann Jane Anderson (nee Garrick) (1876-1919)

My mother was always known as Jeannie. She came from Sandsound and was the eldest of the family. I'm not sure how she met my father. My brother Tom was born before our parents married, presumably because my father was at sea by the time she realised she was pregnant, so marriage had to wait till he returned home. Aged 21 when she married in 1894, over the next twenty-three years she had ten babies, of whom two were stillborn.

In the summer of 1919 she returned home exhausted from a trip to Lerwick, where I believe arrangements had been initiated for her to have an operation in Edinburgh. Lerwick to Slyde was a long, slow journey, lengthened by

Circa 1894: Ann Jane Garrick, known as Jeannie – my mother.

the 'need' for the male passengers in the gig to stop at Huxter, Weisdale, for a drink at the bar. The final part of her journey home was by boat, by which time she was so weak she was carried up to the house. She never recovered and soon afterwards died of kidney failure, aged just 47. According to her death certificate, the cause of death was Bright's Disease. So I have no memory of my mother, as I was only one year 9 months old when she died.

9

Faider

Thomas Anderson (1869-1963)

Regardless of the real relationship, my father was called Faider by all who lived at Slyde.

Faider's Schooldays

I often heard my father tell about one summer's day at school on the Ayre o' Voxter. The minister from Scatsta had come along to inspect the children. When he had finished giving them a bigger going over than usual the minister offered up a prayer to God, giving thanks for the opportunity those children were having by way of getting some education.

Outside the school somewhere was an old tin basin which the boys used to kick around during a short interval for play. Nearby, cows were grazing. Right in the middle of the minister's prayer one of the cows felt a need to obey the call of nature which of course set the children sniggering. The teacher, John Johnson (John o' da Holm), was black affronted! When the prayer was over, he turned to the minister and said, "I must apologise for the children's behaviour; for they paid more attention to Tammie Hall's cow pissin in a tin plate than they listened to your prayer!"

What stories my father could have told; only we neglected to ask. But then, youth is more interested in looking ahead, and by the time one is long past middle age often the old folk who could have told so much have passed on.

After attending John Johnson's 'peerie skules' (more of these later), Faider was a pupil under Mr Allison at Gonfirth for two years, before leaving at the age of 13 in 1882.

It seems that Mr Allison was keen to teach singing, but of course some of the boys (and maybe some girls too) refused to comply; and there would have been those whose vocal chords couldn't even sing the notes on the scale. During those sessions, the teacher would stroll backwards and forwards behind the pupils to discover who was singing and who was not. Faider and his pal, Andrew Tait (from the Haa, East Burrafirth), had decided to remain silent even though both could sing. One afternoon after school time, while guddlin' in the Voxter Burn, they got an idea it would be a good place to raise their voices in song. They were giving it all they had when who appeared above them but their teacher! He, of course, had heard them singing "Ye banks and braes" as well as "Come ower da stream, Charlie". What a firsmo they both got, as you can well imagine, and I expect they may have got the strap, or at least would have been told off, for disobeying their teacher.

Another story from my father's school-days at Gonfirth was how he and another school pal, Walter Balfour from Houbanster, would sometimes manage to capture two year-old oxen which were out on the open scattald (on the loose) trying to fill their bellies with heather and coarse grass. Those animals belonged to the Peterson family, living in one of the croft houses at South Voxter – this family had apparently been evicted from Marrofield shortly before. Anyway, the boys managed to get on to the backs of those oxen and had a minor rodeo on the way home from school! I shouldn't think that the back of an undernourished ox could have made a comfortable seat, though thick worsted drawers and moleskin trousers made good padding! One also wonders what those Peterson women would have thought!

Circa 1894: Thomas Anderson – Faider.

"Sic an onkerry" by those two hooligan schoolboys. But as the old saying goes "Boys will be boys".

When attending all those schools, pupils were expected each to bring one or two big skyumpie peats to help keep a fire going. No peat, no chance to get near the fire on a cold day. I expect the very first parochial schools may have had a fire in the middle of the floor with an opening in the thatched roof to let out the smoke.

Whistling Tom

Faider went herring fishing when he left school. He later sailed as bosun on larger ships. He would have liked to study for his skipper's ticket but with a young family there was no cash to pay for that. He always carried a whistle which he blew whenever he thought the men were slacking – he soon got the nickname Whistling Tom. I remember one time my nephew, George, and I were walking home from Gonfirth when the fog came down, making orientation difficult. Just as we were disagreeing about which way we should be walking, we were very blyde to hear Faider's whistle guiding us homeward. Every house had at least one whistle, with the number and lengths of blasts indicating a variety of messages.

In 1923, my father sustained injuries from a fall into the hold of a ship (at Brest in France), when he broke a leg and both arms. As a result, he had a compensation pension from, I believe, the Shipping Federation. I am not certain how often it was paid, but I remember he received a postal order for £2; I think it might have been fortnightly. Whenever any member of the family went shopping they always took 'Faider's purse' in case the knitting they usually took to barter couldn't pay for all the messages.

Interests

Faider liked to keep up with current affairs. He wrote many letters and was a great reader – he used to say, "It's a poor book dat's no wirt reading." He read anything he could find and when nothing else was available he read the Bible. I remember *Christian Herald, Sunday Companion, Womens' World, News of the World* – some of these would have been a regular order from the shop; others were swopped with neighbours. Library books came in boxes, by boat, to the East Burrafirth School from the late 1920s. These were available for any member of the community to borrow and I well remember Faider's delight when he heard a new box had arrived.

We got a wireless sometime before World War Two but the only programme ever heard was the news, usually once a day, for the accumulator needed to go the Clark & Co. shop at Aith to be charged up – that was a heavy burden and would have cost money too. I'd have liked to listen to the music on Radio Luxembourg or Athlone but that was not allowed!

My father lived to be an old man, but lost his eyesight in his early 90s. He died only a few weeks short of his 94th birthday, in 1963.

1955: Slyde. Faider, Tom Anderson, aged 86.

10
Auntie Ellen

Helen Anderson (nee Garrick) (1881-1952)

My mother's sister, Ellen, had married one of my father's brothers, Robbie, in 1905. She had come to live at Slyde when she married and no doubt my mother would have been glad of the company. Her son Peter was born in November 1906, and her husband was lost at sea in June 1907, never having been home to see his son. There was no widow's pension in those days so Auntie Ellen stayed at Slyde and Peter was brought up along with our family. When our mother died in 1919, Auntie Ellen was there, keeping the family together. When Auntie Ellen did eventually get a widow's pension – ten shillings a week – the first week's pension went into the collection plate at Gonfirth chapel.

1934: Auntie Ellen and the author.

Auntie Ellen was very reticent and didn't divulge much family history. She was a hard worker herself, and constantly urged me to keep busy. When Peter married she moved with him and his wife to Tumblin, where she died aged 71, having lived longer than any of her siblings.

11
Tom and Davie

TOM and Davie were the oldest and youngest of my five brothers. Tom, like Jeemie and Johnnie, was away in the Merchant Navy before I can remember. They came home for a spell each year but I was not of their age group, so didn't know them too well.

1916: Tom Anderson.

1924: Davie Anderson, aged 13.

Family tragedy

On Thursday, 18th April, 1929, a family tragedy came as a great shock to our household at Slyde. Tom, aged 34, and Davie, aged 17, lost their lives in a boating accident not far from our home – just across at the back of Aithsness. They were on their way to the Aith Shop in a lug sail boat. I was 11½ years old at the time, too young to feel the full force of the shock which the adults had to bear.

I remember that afternoon and evening clearly. After school I had been sent to Skeetalea for a head (four hanks) of yarn (it was a common practice to borrow and repay neighbours). The men had had an early tea by the time I got home. Mimie and John Robert had gone to Briggidale to meet the mobile shop van from Tagon but I don't remember where George was. Liza had gone to Lochside for a few days as our aunt was unwell, and I believe she expected to meet Tom and Davie at the shop, to sell the hosiery they would bring, and then come home with them. Tom had gone to get the boat ready and Davie set off as Maggie and I washed dishes. I remember Auntie Ellen signalling to Davie to come back for Faider's purse.

Then the postman arrived. He came only as far as the hill daek then blew his whistle and waited for someone to walk up the hill to fetch the mail. I was sent to collect the mail – a parcel containing dresses (ordered from either J. D. Williams or Oxendales) for the family wedding planned for the following month. I couldn't wait to open the parcel and in moments was changed into my beige dress and admiring myself in a small mirror. My sister Maggie's blue dress was the same as mine. Auntie Ellen soon had me back in the usual clothes as she needed to wind the yarn I'd just brought for her, and I held the hank for her. She wound the yarn with my niece, Jean, sitting on her knee. More than once she said, "Look if du sees da boat," but I saw no boat. Once the hank had been wound I went down to the Nort Ayre and played there for a while.

In the meantime, Faider was preparing for voar by digging out the lamb house, keeping his eye on the sea each time he went out with a barrowload of muck. Once he looked and saw they were about to tack; next time they'd disappeared – he immediately suspected what had happened.

When I walked back up to the house I saw Faider and Auntie Ellen standing in the door with spy glasses. I was still too young to figure out what was going on, and I guess they tried to protect me from picking up on their anxiety. Mimie and John Robert returned. Mimie wishfully thought that they'd gone round Papa Little.

No other adult male was at Slyde that afternoon so Faider set off on foot to our neighbours at Skeetalea. He and John used their boat to row to the area where our boat was last seen. As the evening wore on, the wind fell away and it became a fine night. When Faider and John came back, Faider immediately went to the Wasthoose to ask Jeemie to tell the Hametoon folk the news. Jeemie did as he was asked and returned with Mootie ("Jeemie said I wid hae ta go, bit I didna want ta go"). There was lots of coming and going that night. Mr Bennie, the Church of Scotland missionary in Aith, went to Lochside to tell Liza.

Next day, Maggie and I, not knowing how to deal with these circumstances, spent most of the day in bed. I remember Baabie and Geordie Nicolson coming from Scalloway – their son John tells me one of his earliest memories is of his fury at knowing that they were going to Slyde without him. I also remember Ellen Tait arriving from Braewick with black sateen peenies for Maggie and me. These were decorated at the neck with black French knots, had elbow length sleeves and gathered waists. I don't know if she'd sewed them overnight.

Gales prevented searches the following two days; an attempt on the Saturday afternoon had to be abandoned. On Sunday a large number of boats, including five or six from Burra, plus a diver, came and searched without success; my father used a water glass for the search. A water glass is a square wooden box with a glass bottom and open top. The sides would have been 2-3 feet deep so that it could go below the waves. It was used to see what was on the sea bottom.

On Monday the gale blew again. The remote possibility of them absconding to another land was soon discovered not possible as on Tuesday my father found the wreck of their boat on the banks of Aith Voe. It was this fact that confirmed that they had indeed been lost. Davie's body was also found. Tom's body was not recovered in spite of extensive searching.

Tom's marriage to Nannie Tait (Hametoon) had been planned for sometime in May, that same year, so the tragic accident cast a deep gloom, not only in our home, but also over the whole district.

What had happened to them one will never know. As with every young man of the day, both were trained and well used to life at sea, and hence were experienced sailors. The cause of many an accident is a flan of wind or a freak wave, however neither is likely to cause a boat to capsize in a small sheltered inlet. My father spent most Sundays that summer prowling the shores of Aith Voe. Over the years the story of the weather condition on that day has varied, but none has said that it was a rough day. Calm and foggy is the most common, and the most likely, hence why nobody onshore would have seen anything.

When Tom and Davie left Slyde that day they'd had a parcel of hosiery to trade at the shop in Aith – knitwear at that time was always bartered for shop goods. It had been carefully parcelled for the trip and when the boat sank it floated ashore somewhere near Skeetalea. John Eunson had retrieved it and taken it to their house. It was my sad task to go there to collect the parcel – its contents were certainly far too valuable to abandon.

Robbie and our cousin, Peter, were sailing in the Far East at this time. At one port one of their shipmates, from Scalloway, found his mail included at least one issue of *The Shetland Times*. Once the ship had set sail again, he read of the tragedy but did not share the news with Robbie and Peter until they were approaching their next port of call, which I think must have been in the UK, for they immediately travelled home. On arriving in Lerwick they took a taxi, getting out at Briggidale so they could walk over the hill to Slyde without meeting the neighbours. With not a sign of habitation, the driver couldn't believe this was the nearest he could take them to home! I remember the surprise of their arrival, just as we were leaving for school.

Mourning

What I remember most from that time is the wearing of black clothes. Two of our cousins – Clark & Co.'s dyers – came and began to boil up black dye in the big pot which was used only for the dyeing of yarn, to knit those popular all-over Fair Isle jumpers which had become high fashion in the early 1920s. Well, all our outerwear went into that black dye, including the outfits we'd just got to wear at Tom's wedding.

For the previous Christmas Liza had knitted Maggie and me wine coloured pleated skirts with matching jumpers. The jumpers were decorated at the neck with embroidered flowers. While the dye was prepared I was given a pair of scissors and asked to cut the flowers off the jumper before it was dyed. How I gowled – but I was gowling more for the loss of the flowers than for the loss of brothers who were so much older than me!

The men didn't have to dress in black – they just wore black ties. I wished I was a man! Faider refused to get a new black hat for the funeral. Our shoes for Tom and Nannie's wedding arrived in early May – they were brown, which I thought was splendid, till they too got dyed black. I remember going to a picnic and afterwards heard John Robert say, "I could aesy see Chrissie fir sho wis da onnly een wearin' black." I didn't like the attention it attracted. Even at Liza's wedding, almost three years later, I wore a black long-sleeved dress trimmed with black lace collar and cuffs. At that time families had to wear those black clothes; I suppose Queen Victoria had much to do with it. I hated it, I could see no sense in having to do so, but I was overruled. We wore that dismal colour for three years, almost. Then we went from black to navy blue, and dark greys; it was a long time before we eventually ended up wearing any bright colours. When I was old enough to order my own new dress it was bright red – even then I couldn't escape attention for I heard it said, "She's fairly come oot o da black."

The youth of today wear black because it may be fashionable – but not so when I was a child. I know of women who were widowed while still young and they wore black for the rest of their lives! All supposed to show respect for the dead in the family. What a load of nonsense!

12

Robbie (1896-1984) and Mimie (1895-1977)

ONE of my earliest memories, in August 1920, is when my brother Robbie married Mimie Tait from Hametoon. Our brother Johnnie was best man. I remember going to the Hametoon to await the return of the bridal party –

1948: Robbie and Mimie Anderson.

they had married in Lerwick. Everyone was waiting to see them come across the voe by boat but I was much more interested in the bride's four-week-old baby niece – the first baby I had ever seen!

Robbie and Mimie moved into our house. Their elder son, John Robert, was born in 1921 and became the close companion of my childhood and youth; he was much closer than any of my own brothers who were so much older than me. My sister-in-law Mimie was good to me, explaining things which in my childish mind were sometimes hard to understand. Two more children were born to Robbie and Mimie: George in 1925 and Jean in 1928. I

January 1940: John Robert –
Robbie and Mimie's elder son.

1943: Jean aged 14, with her mother, Mimie.

1936: at Houbinster. John Nicolson (Baabie's son) and George Anderson (Robbie and Mimie's younger son) – two little mischief makers. John came to Slyde every summer for holidays. He and George were the same age; they were like chalk and cheese but usually got on well, but George could fairly wind up the hasty tempered John. One memorable time they fell out whilst off fishing from a boat, so they came ashore, made the boat fast, then started to fight, out of sight of the grown-ups at the house.
Debateless, they made it to the house saying, "Nixt time we fecht we'll need a referee."

1959: Robbie, Faider and Mimie outside Slyde.

53

can remember Maggie, John Robert, George and I playing in the washhouse whilst Mimie gave birth – I hadn't noticed any sign of a baby's imminent arrival though might have guessed as Auntie Meggie had come to stay.

In 1931, Mimie needed treatment in hospital. I remember her return, about a week before her sister (Betty) died following childbirth. She came by boat to the pier at Slyde. Robbie and Lollie (her brother) made a chair with their arms and carried her up to the house. Faider, trying to help clear the path for them, kicked a box out of the way, but he'd forgotten that this was the bottomless box where John Robert kept his guinea pig, regularly moving him to fresh pasture. There was consternation over this for the guinea pig had escaped among the tatties! I don't remember if he was ever found again.

Robbie was always able to answer many of my questions about local and family history – how I wish I'd asked him much more. I have many pleasant memories of Robbie and all his family.

13

Jeemie (1900-1975)

LIKE Tom, Jeemie was away in the Merchant Navy before I can remember. He enjoyed a fairly long retirement in Shetland so that's really when I got to know him.

Jeemie appears to have been a very reluctant scholar. After spending his very early years playing mostly with peerie home-made wooden boats in da dukes' loch, he fairly kicked up a dust when it became clear that he would have to attend school. Jeemie was 17 years older than me so his schooldays were well and truly over by the time I was born. I remember my older brother Robbie tell how he had to carry Jeemie on his back to the school which was in the ben-end of the Upper Pund, East Burrafirth, where the teacher was a young woman called Jane Ann. Robbie was of slender build while Jeemie was round and fat so, though four years older than Jeemie, I imagine it would have been a sair fecht. Our mother, or one of the other adults at Slyde, would accompany the boys part of the way. But Jeemie, being of stubborn nature, wanted to turn back, so, poor boy, he got lifted on to Robbie's back. Tom, our eldest brother, had by this time gone to Gonfirth School and Robbie followed soon after.

The very first day that Jeemie was carried to school at Jane Ann's house he refused to enter the seat of learning. As the old proverb says "You can lead a horse to water but you can't make him drink". This surely could have been applied to Jeemie as he sat on the floor behind the outer door among some empty jam jars. Jane Ann's mother produced a wooden spoon, so there Jeemie sat stirring among those jars. I daresay he would have run home fast enough when the time came.

Many stories were told of Jeemie's misbehaviour and lack of co-operation with his teachers. One eventful afternoon, after he had progressed from Jane Ann's school, he had disobeyed his teacher who was one who believed that to spare the rod would spoil the child! Jeemie was told to come out before his teacher and hold out his hand. He refused to obey, so the teacher grabbed hold and, laying him across his knees, proceeded to give Jeemie a good wallop over his backside with a cane. I daresay, in Jeemie's childish mind, there came a need to retaliate, so he used the only method he could think of – he opened his mouth as wide as it could go and sank his teeth into his teacher's limb. "Oh, you little devil, you!" Losing his grip on Jeemie's shoulders for an instant, he gave his pupil enough time to make a bolt for the door, where he skulked out

of sight outside until it was time to join the others at home time. The other boys admired Jeemie's courage! But our mother apparently gave her wayward son a bit of timely advice: "Teachers must always be obeyed – or else." Anyway, after that incident, a silent compromise was reached between Jeemie and his teacher. "You beat me; I bite you!" It had been a come-down for both teacher and pupil – in front of all the other children, too.

Jeemie married Mary Tait from Braewick, Aith, in 1923. I was recovering from whooping cough so wasn't at their wedding. They had a son, Tom, and daughter, Wilma. They moved away from Shet-land but it was not a happy

Circa 1930: Jeemie Anderson and his wife, Mary (nee Tait) – photo taken in South Shields.

marriage and they eventually divorced – quite unusual in those days. When Jeemie retired, he returned to Shetland and stayed for a time with Mary's sister and her family at Ellsemere House in Lerwick, until he moved to the Walter and Joan Gray Eventide Home in Scalloway. Jeemie loved to sing and was full of fun, and at times could fairly put on a comic act and enjoyed having a fun with the staff there. He died in 1975.

Mary remarried but she and I exchanged letters until she died, in California, in 2005.

14

Johnnie (1902-1970)

JOHNNIE also went to sea and was rarely home when I was a bairn. He was best man at Robbie and Mimie's wedding. I'm not sure, but I think he went away about 1921 and didn't come home till 1929, after our brothers died. Jobs for seamen weren't then plentiful so perhaps he couldn't afford to come home. He spent a lot of shore leave in South Shields with our Uncle Joseph who had settled there. I remember him coming home with Auntie Lillie from South Shields in 1932.

He must have come home more often after that because in 1936 he married Mary Ann Tait, from Upper Pund, East Burrafirth. They married at the Sand Manse and I was their bridesmaid. It was a fine April

1932: Johnnie and the author.

night and I remember Mary Ann's mother and Mimie o' Slyde were in charge of tea-making on a fire outside; inside John Robertson sat on the dresser playing the fiddle for the dancers.

Johnnie and Mary Ann spent most of their married life in Upper Pund and had three daughters – Wilma, Margaret and Joyce. Illness overtook Johnnie and he didn't enjoy a very long retirement.

1936: wedding photo of Johnnie Anderson and Mary Ann Tait, with Tammie Jacobson (bride's cousin) and the author.

15
Eliza (1905-1982)

MY eldest sister, whose name was always shortened to Liza, was 12 years my senior. She was always a grown-up in my memory

She married Lollie Tait (Hametoon) on 8th March, 1932. They, too, married in Lerwick. Our cousin Peter was best man and Lollie's sister Nannie was bridesmaid. A car took them from Lerwick to Hestataing where Faider was waiting to take them to Slyde by boat – Liza, wearing her long satin dress and veil, with a coat over her shoulders. As she stepped onto the pier, I noticed she wore a pair of old shoes and carried her white wedding shoes. They were lucky the weather was fair – dry and not much wind. Nannie wore a beige dress and black hat.

Liza's good friend, Ellen, had come from Braewick to help with the wedding meal – this was the first time I'd seen a tin of assorted fancy biscuits. Lollie's sisters, Mootie and Babsy, with nieces and nephews, had come from the Hametoon and brought a pound of rice to throw over the newlyweds when we met them at the pier – but Auntie Ellen thought that a waste of good food! One of Lollie's young nieces had swallowed a halfpenny that morning, so some of the adults were on the lookout for its reappearance!

Liza moved from Slyde into the Hametoon. After she left I must have been pooskin around when I found two books which were so well thumbed that the covers had come off. One was an illustrated book on childbirth which Liza took to the Hametoon once she realised she was pregnant. The other was a sexual science book which had no pictures but plenty to read, including the advice "never give yourself to any man till after you are married" so I decided to follow that, for doing otherwise seemed likely to be troublesome. I was given no advice to read the books and often wonder where they had come from.

Liza and Lollie had six children – Laurence, Tammie, Bobby, Bertie, Jeannie and Elma. Liza was very house-proud, unlike me, who was more of a dreamer and reader. After she married, I would often be reminded: "I ken Liza wid a hed da stove brushed an' shinin'." After she moved out I was the one who went shopping to Gudataing, or to Gonfirth, or to meet vans etc. There was no end to what needed doing, including big washings and ironings every week.

By the time Liza and I were grandmothers ourselves, I remember Liza recalling one of her contemporaries who'd gone to Up-Helly-A' as a

Wedding photo – Liza and Lollie Tait.

teenager. Nine months later she was needing ante-natal care, so she asked the doctor how long getting pregnant took, as her "sister hed been oot far laanger wi her een as I wis wi my een." His answer was, "About as long as it takes to peel a potato." So now you know!

Another woman she spoke of had become pregnant to a married man, so there was no chance of getting married to the father. Her parents put her out and she found life tough for her and her son. She managed to find work as a live-in housekeeper for a man who was living on his own in the usual basic accommodation. She surely decided an alliance with him would give her security but he wasn't biting the usual bait, so more drastic action was

August 1928: Robbie, Peter and Liza.

required! She and her young son slept in the top tier of a wooden box bed, her employer on the lower deck. Each day she sawed at the wood a little, till eventually, one night, her weight brought her and her son down into his bed. He wondered what he was to do as there was no other bed in the house; so she "telled him ta lie whaar he wis." They went on to get married, and had three daughters together. I'd like to say they lived happily ever after, but she didn't treat him very lovingly and the neighbours often felt sorry for him.

I have happy memories of Liza enjoying our Ruby Wedding celebration, but she took a heavy stroke and died shortly after.

16
Maggie (1913-2007)

MY other sister, Maggie, was "different" – nowadays some fancy name would be given, most likely something in the autistic range. As an infant it was said that Maggie cried a lot and was not an easy child to get settled to sleep; as an adult she was very placid, easy to please and very, very rarely lost her temper. She liked things to be orderly – one thing she hated was sheep caain, probably because of the noise and the chaos! She played her part in our household, where everyone had their own daily chores as well as helping with the seasonal tasks.

Maggie learned to knit before she went to school; she was a beautiful knitter. She never sat 'haand idle' so knitted while listening to everything the older folk were speaking about, and years later could write down exactly what Auntie Ellen had said, what Mimie had said, also what everybody else had said; the exact date; even the exact hour! For years she knitted Fair Isle gloves which contributed to what the household had to barter at the shop. She gave up knitting on her 80th birthday as that was when her grandmother gave up knitting.

Maggie attended the East Burrafirth school. It says much for her teacher that Maggie learned to read and write; she probably wouldn't have fitted in at a bigger school where she would not have got such individual attention. On Sunday afternoons – always a day of rest – Maggie spent hours reading, often a dictionary. She acquired a huge vocabulary and learned the meanings, if not the pronunciation, of many words, having an alert, enquiring brain.

She had an incredibly retentive memory for dates – whether it be someone's birthday and their age, or a date when something unusual happened – and could repeat conversations overheard in the distant past. She learned long poems by heart and on many occasions recited these from memory. I often requested this on our long walks together.

Sometimes she came out with some fair wisecracks, saying things which raised many a laugh. Hearing others discuss a pregnancy, she said, "I tocht Lollie (the expectant father) wisna been hame." In jest, Auntie Ellen replied, "Jeemie o' da Haa is no far awa," to which Maggie retorted, "I didna tink dey threw germ whin dey cam sae aald." Another time, Maggie's response to someone asking "Will da lads ever win here?" was, "Laek dugs, dey ey win whar dey want ta win." I cannot remember her ever saying or doing anything which hurt anybody's feelings.

In the past, people didn't speak about the people who'd died, often totally avoiding using their names, so Mimie's nieces were grateful to Maggie for her willingness to speak to them about their mother, who'd died before they were old enough to remember her. No doubt the elders would have put a stop to that if they'd heard her.

The young folk gradually moved out and Slyde became home to just four – Maggie, our father, our brother Robbie, and his wife Mimie. Our father died in 1963 and Mimie died in 1977. That left just Maggie and Robbie, by then aged 63 and 80. They moved from Slyde to live with Robbie's daughter, Jean, and her family in Lerwick. Maggie adapted well to life in the centre of town, but particularly enjoyed day trips back to Slyde. Jean had a schoolboy lodger who was aware that Maggie sometimes looked in his room. To discourage this as tactfully as he could, he put his things in a box and labelled it 'explosives'. Her reaction was to question the advisability of having explosives in the house!

Maggie loved cats, and always called her cat her "faithful friend". I made a point of sending her a card and a peerie letter every fortnight, always enclosing pictures of a cat or two. I'm told that Maggie kept all those cards I sent standing on a deep window sill, and took them down every day to re-read and study those lovely pictures of kittens. She also loved her birthdays, and Christmas, for that meant gifts.

In 1981, following Jean's death, Maggie and Robbie moved to Burra to stay with Robbie's son, George, and his family. Again Maggie adapted very well to the move, as well as the changes that family deaths meant. Eventually, just

George and Maggie shared the house, but they got on well together and he often referred to her as his "computer" for she could supply him with so much detailed information on many a subject from the past. Maggie accepted all the changes as "da wye o things".

After George's death, in 1999, his family were happy for her to remain in their family home, accepting respite care for her at the Walter and Joan Gray Home in Scalloway several times a year. Maggie was very happy staying there, though by this time was too deaf to hear conversation. Communication was on paper – a question was asked and frequently answered in writing, as she had been taught at school, in a full sentence with correct punctuation. Maggie benefited greatly from the constant care of George's daughter, Barbara, as well as the work of home helps, care assistants, nurses and doctors, and always appreciated the help she was given. As the carer left, Maggie said, "Thank you very, very, very, very much. Thank you is poor pay but better than saying nothing at all."

Maggie enjoyed good health for most of her life. Apart from deafness, she suffered from glaucoma and twice travelled to Aberdeen to have treatment on her eyes. Like me, I'm sure she enjoyed a life of ease after all the hard work of her youth. She fairly enjoyed her stays in Scalloway, and at Bannamin she had a great deal of support and kind consideration from George's family. She died at Walter & Joan Gray Eventide Home on Friday, 26th January, 2007.

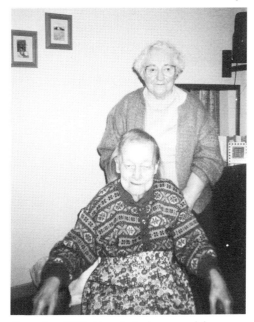

December 1999: Maggie Anderson and the author at Walter and Joan Gray Eventide Home, Scalloway. When this was taken it was probably fifty years since the sisters had been photographed together.

17
Peter (1906-1978)

PETER, my double cousin (Auntie Ellen's son), was eleven years older than me. He grew up at Slyde and was like another big brother. He too went into the Merchant Navy. We became much closer after I became an adult.

In 1932, not long after Liza married, the postman asked Robbie, "Ir you gottin ony wird fae Peter?" It seemed a curious question, but the postman had surely heard that some of Peter's shipmates had died following an outbreak of smallpox on board the ship. Peter, at that time, was sailing somewhere out east. He was old enough to have had the compulsory smallpox vaccination when he was young so escaped that fate. By my time it was no longer given.

Peter played a large part in my life in the first half of 1935, when he was aged about 29. In January, he went to Lerwick Up-Helly-A'. At the beginning of February there was a dance at Cole – da Cole Up-Helly-A' – which we attended. I remember coming home about six in the morning to find Willie o' da Hametoon waiting for Peter to join him for a day's fishing. So, without having any sleep, Peter set off, but really wasn't well when he got home. Next day the postman arrived with news that a few young folk had got measles and when Peter heard the names he realised he'd shared transport with them at the end of January. He, too, had measles but was sufficiently ill that Dr MacKenzie – a new young doctor based in Walls – was sent for. He diagnosed pneumonia as well as measles. Poultices on the chest were required for Peter's pneumonia – I don't remember whether these were mustard or kaolin.

Auntie Ellen must have been staying with one of her sisters when Peter became ill, for on her return to East Burrafirth, as she didn't think she'd had measles, she slept at the Hametoon till we'd all recovered. Mimie's sister (Maggie) came from Burra to help out as by this time the younger members of the Slyde household also had measles. I remember my sister Maggie, and I, in one bedroom which was cold and draughty. A fire was lit in the grate but no-one knew that Auntie Ellen had stuffed an old pair of trousers up the chimney to stop some of the draughts. This, of course, started a chimney fire – frightening at the best of times. My sister Maggie was most upset by being ill, and the fire, and it took her some time to recover. Faider came upstairs with toddy to bring the measles out, but I had a very light dose so endured them a second time over forty years later, and disliked whisky ever since. In addition to the Slyde folk getting measles, Peter had, of course, spread the infection to young and old who were at the Cole dance, so he was not too popular that voar!

Not long afterwards, Peter got a motorcycle which he kept in one of the outbuildings at Hestataing. He had an accident in April 1935, somewhere about Pund, Aith, when he required some first aid to his head. I was collecting in the area (house-to-house collections were then undertaken quite regularly for one charity or another) and surprised the occupants of the Pund by turning up there just as someone was tending to Peter's wounds. He was able to get back to Slyde, accompanied by me, so the injuries surely weren't too serious – I think he had a bandage round his head, and I remember stopping along the Hametoon on the way home.

In June 1935, I had been to a Rechabite picnic somewhere about Bixter. In the early evening I was at the Hametoon, on my way home, when we noticed unusual boat activity between Slyde and Hestataing/Scarvataing. Mootie guessed something had happened to Peter and his bike! Liza and I set off for Slyde where we learned that Peter had had an accident. Faider was saying, "He'll be unconscious," which annoyed Mimie, who didn't care to hear such words.

Peter had been on the way home, between Annesville and Scarvataing, when he met animals on the road. Swerving to avoid them, him and bike left the road and his head hit a large stone at the upper side of the road. He managed to walk to Scarvataing before losing consciousness. Someone must have gone to Aith to phone for the doctor and/or ambulance; someone else must have been despatched to Slyde to report the news to the family. Willie o' Pirliegert was also summoned, as he had a little first aid knowledge through being on the lifeboat.

Peter's mother, Auntie Ellen, was staying with her sister in Sandsound at the time so next day I was sent to tell her the news. Several men in Aith had a hiring business so I travelled by car. I forget now how we organised this transport – probably someone cycled to the driver's house. I wasn't the only passenger for I remember Katie Leask from Houster coming too, and she went to visit her future in-laws up the hill from my relatives in Sandsound.

When I got to Sandsound, Auntie Ellen was baking, but she stopped immediately and gathered together a few necessities before we walked back up the hill to the waiting car. We were taken straight to the hospital where the matron came out to warn us that Peter's head injuries were very serious and he was still unconscious. We were allowed to see him briefly before leaving to seek accommodation with Annie Mouat, a family friend, as the hospital staff were anxious to know where Auntie Ellen could be found. This was my first experience of being in a hospital.

I stayed in Lerwick with Auntie Ellen for a night or two. Another new experience was going to the Post Office to use the telephone for the first time, to send news of Peter to Aith Post Office – the only phone in the area.

Peter was in hospital for about three weeks but afterwards made a good recovery, with only a scar on his temple as a reminder.

Peter was in the merchant service when war broke out. At one point he sailed on an Australian ship; on the voyage immediately after he left the ship, she was lost with all hands. Later in the war he drove a dumper in the building of the airport at Scatsta.

Peter – Auntie Ellen's son.

Like his Slyde cousins Robbie and Liza, Peter married one of the Hametoon family, Babsy, in 1944. They moved to a small croft in Tumblin. Although they had no family they were always blyde to see the young folk and many of their nieces and nephews went there for holidays.

Babsy died first and, as Peter's health failed, he spent more time with Jeemie and I at Hestataing, where he died in 1978.

Peter – Auntie Ellen's son, a bit older.

Section 3

Early Life

18

School Days

I DO not know the exact date I started school but I think it would have been after the Easter holidays in 1924. Mostly all children in our area had had a prolonged bout of whooping-cough during the winter of 1923, followed in February by a very virulent type of flu which laid low whole households; and in this district alone five elderly folk died of it, including my grandmother at Slyde.

Both these epidemics had apparently left me in poor shape. I had lost weight so, to boost my general health, bottles of tonic by the name of Scott's Emulsion were bought from the Aith shop and spooned regularly each day into my mouth. I assume the basic ingredient would have been cod-liver oil laced with some nicer tasting concoction to mask the oily taste. I recall that the trade-mark on the bottle was a fisherman dressed in oilskins and sou'wester, carrying a huge fish tied with a thin rope through its gills and hanging down the fisherman's back. Luckily, I loved the taste of the stuff so took it without kicking up any fuss.

Although Slyde lies out of sight of the rest of East Burrafirth, the journey to school took only about fifteen minutes when walking, and less time if one felt like running. There was a sort of 'trukkit gaet' up from our house to the Sooth Grind, then a flattish part before we gained Da Wasthoose Grind, then down hill until we came to the Mill Burn.

That burn could carry a fair amount of water after heavy rain; its source was Da Loch o' Burrafirth. Long before my time it had driven a water-mill, situated not all that far up from the crofts. There's little sign now that a mill ever existed, for when a road got laid in through East Burrafirth the stones from the mill were taken to build a bridge – no thoughts of conservation existed in those days. It was away with the old and on with the new.

There were stepping stones laid across the burn at its widest section – just a short way from our school. I was nervous about crossing them when only the tops were showing above the racing water; but help was usually at hand. Babsy Tait from Hametoon would be standing by to grasp small hands and swing us safely across. Babsy was school cleaner and got a good peat fire going before the pupils arrived.

2007: on the extreme left is the burn we had to cross to get to school – also where we washed our slates and answered the call of nature. What's left of the East Burrafirth school – just the walls – is immediately right of the burn; next right is the Hametoon; the Haa is no longer there and on the far right of the photo is the East Gate where Faider was born.

My teacher, Agnes (Nannie) Tait

In 1915, Nannie Tait from the Hametoon was asked whether she would consider taking on the job of teaching those younger children at East Burrafirth. Nannie, born in 1899, a daughter of Laurie and Baabie Tait, had attended Gonfirth school and on leaving in 1913 had gone straight to work at the Post Office at Voe. Anyway, she responded to the call and began what seemingly fate had ordained – a long teaching career.

By the time Nannie took over teaching, most of the bigger boys had left school so maybe her task proved easier than it might have a few years earlier.

Nannie was a disciplinarian by nature. She seemed capable of keeping her brother and sisters in their place as well as children, yet she didn't rule by fear. Usually, when any of us didn't toe the line, it took only a look and a few words from our teacher to let us know where we stood!

Nannie Tait was a good teacher, in spite of the fact that she had had no training for such a job. Besides teaching us most subjects, except music, she taught us the true worth of honesty and truthfulness.

She had become engaged to my eldest brother Tom and their wedding date had been set for sometime in May 1929. It was a hard blow when Tom lost his life, but Nannie resumed her teaching duties a week or two after the Easter holidays.

The school building

The schoolroom at East Burrafirth was in what, I assume, would have been the ben-end of the original house. It had a strong wooden floor and was also wood-lined. Being about 12 feet by 14 feet (3.6m x 4.3m approximately) in size, it was quite a cosy place.

Agnes (Nannie) Tait – teacher at East Burrafirth from about 1917 till about 1942.

There were three skylights – one of which could open – and a small window on the front wall facing south. When I first remember it the only door opened right from outside into the schoolroom. It was not until around 1930 that an inside porch was built, fitted with double coat hooks.

An upended orange box served as a washstand on which there was room for an enamel basin and soap dish. An enamel ewer stood on the shelf below, always half full of clean water. I suppose there would have been a towel as well. We eventually progressed to a circular iron washstand which we thought a great advancement. In spite of all those facilities, sometimes I was too lazy to bother washing my hands. When they got too grimy I had a habit of licking the balls of my thumbs and giving a hasty rub on the sides of my peenie. So much for hygiene!

A door just inside the outer door, set into the wooden partition, led into the room at the west end of the building. This place was referred to as 'da black end' – possibly because there never seemed to be much light; I don't remember it having a skylight. It had an earthen floor, and that's where the school's peats, cut and cured by the Hametoon family, were stored.

The peat banks in those days were quite some way up the hill, near the Loch o' Burrafirth and Longawater – there was no road there. The Hametoon folk had a small chestnut pony named Rosie who got fitted out with harness for pulling a sledge. That was the method used to transport maybe six or eight bags of peat from the peat banks down to the hill-daek where a big stack was built. That was still quite some way up from the houses and the school, where at the start of each session there was always a good heap of peats in da black end. Whether someone had humped them down on their backs or not, I have not yet discovered. Da face o' da Gerts was certainly too steep for a pony harnessed to a sledge. I have been told that after the road in through East Burrafirth got laid a certain amount of coal was supplied to the school, by the Education Department, I assume.

In all the years I attended school there was never any lavatory – not even a dry closet with a bucket, which a cleaner would have had to empty every afternoon. No, we were nearer to earth than that. The arrangement was that whenever a need arose to spend a penny, always during lesson time, you would raise a hand, "Please Miss, can I get out?" Never more than one at a time, under a broo in the nearby burn, we communed at peace with nature.

In summer, docken blades did as toilet roll, but my memory lets me down as to what happened during the winter time. We certainly knew nothing (at least I didn't) of joining a queue to enter a smelly old bucket lavatory. We were used to primitive conditions. What one has never had, one never misses! Anyway, I think it would have been in the summer holidays of 1932 (I had left school in 1931) when men employed by ZCC (Zetland County Council) came to East Burrafirth and erected a wooden lean-to lavatory on the west gable of the school.

Occasionally our slates needed to be cleaned, so on a fine day we washed them in the burn – a handy multi-purpose facility!

The first stove that I can remember was of a round bogey type which had a longish pipe affair which fitted into a throat-plate at the gable. When that one fell apart, another different sort of stove was installed. Sometimes, in dead calm conditions, our small schoolroom would fill with paet-reek which could sting our eyes; but we were never to endure that for long, for our teacher took us outside where there was a long bench on which we sat and read to ourselves, until the all-clear was given.

On that small stove stood a pan with a lid in which water was boiled for making cocoa, to have with our piece at our dinner break. Any child who lived near went home for something to eat. Our teacher always went along to Hametoon, where she lived with other members of her family. Our piece was usually a fair sized flour bannock which had been split sandwich fashion and spread with fresh home churned butter and maybe a trace of rhubarb jam, or maybe two big biscuits stuck together with butter. I seem unable to recall exactly the brand; but it certainly wasn't a Wagonwheel or a Penguin!

Visit from a mouse

All my trying to remember about cocoa and bannocks brings to mind one forenoon shortly after starting school. I was sitting at the end of a long desk, supposed to be trying to do a simple sum on my slate, when I became aware of a quick movement only a few feet away from where I sat. It was only a mouse, emerging from a tiny hole in the skirting board, right down at the floor. My heart gave a leap and I daresay my pale face took on a more ashen hue. He darted up among the children's coats which were hanging on nearby nails, one above the other and mine was lowermost. I sat, petrified, unable to utter a sound, nor to get on to do my sums. By and by the mouse reappeared. This time he sat down on his haunches and cleaned up his whiskers before scuttling back from whence he had come.

Nannie must have noticed my white face and lack of attention to my sums. She said, "Well, Chrissie, are you having trouble?"

I got up enough breath to whisper, "Please, Miss, I saw a mouse."

"A mouse! Where did you see a mouse?"

When I let her know, she got up and inspected the small hole near the floor and from her desk produced a bottle cork which she stuck in the opening – until a proper job was made to debar Mr Mouse! But worse was to come; for when my sister Maggie went to get our piece from the pocket of her coat, lo and behold, all she found was a torn paper bag containing only a few crumbs, and quite a few moose pirls. Silly muggins here began to weep and wail – probably the reaction of shock as well for the loss of our lunch. I never could eat much in the mornings and looked forward to my bannock and my cup of cocoa. But, all was not lost, because Maggie and I were taken down to the Hametoon and we got bread from there.

I have another lovely memory from later. Nannie's older sister, Betty, married with a young family, also lived at Hametoon and often, during our play hour, she would appear at the gable of their byre and signal to me to come (all on the quiet). She took me into the house where she had a plate of lovely soup, all ready on the table for me to sup. I feel ashamed now that I never even thought to say a word of thanks; though I perhaps did repay her in a tacit sort of way by helping take in a bucket of water for her, or on Saturdays keeping an eye on her bairns when I became older.

Sometimes, on the way home, we called at the Holm, where Willie and Teelie (Matilda) Couper lived for a time. We were grateful for the thick chunk of bread Matilda always gave us. Sadly, neither Teelie nor their baby survived a difficult childbirth in April 1930. She was aged about 40. Willie left the Holm then and moved back to live with his mother in Voe – he later re-married and had three children.

I'm side-tracking again, but the next inhabitants of the Holm were Betty and Willie Tait, who had moved from the Hametoon with their five children. Betty died four weeks later. I still remember Betty's kindness when I was a schoolgirl and was greatly saddened when she died in 1931, aged only 40.

About two weeks later the motherless children went down with whooping cough – Auntie Ellen went there overnight to help look after the youngsters, especially the six-week-old baby.

I have been asked by a younger generation, "Who cared for those motherless children?" In those days, when often three generations dwelt under the same roof, a grandmother, aunts and uncles all helped each other. That happened in many a household – even when children had lost both parents there was always somebody ready to take them into their homes. Most folk were compassionate and kind. There may have been parents who were hard-hearted too, or maybe inconsiderate towards their own offspring, especially if they were the sort who show favouritism. Others could have felt jealous and neglected. Human nature sometimes being what it is leaves much to be desired.

After those two deaths people believed the Holm to be an ill-lucked house. Nevertheless, Mootie (from the Upper Pund) and Johnnie Henry moved in, and their two boys, Kenny and Douglas, were born with no mishaps. Johnnie was an agent for Prudential Insurance. He had to row across to Selkieburn, where he kept a motorbike, before he could start his rounds. They later moved to Sandsound so getting to work would have been much easier for him.

Back to my schooldays! When we got home from school in the afternoons there was always part of the grown-ups' dinner awaiting us, kept warm (in an enamel bowl covered by a plate) in the oven of our stove. Very often it would be some lovely mealy tatties with a few cuts of salt herrings or dried salt fish, or sometimes it would have been good thick tattie soup. A cup of milk washed down the tatties and fish. I always hated milk with cream so mine had to come from the jug of skimmed milk. Somehow, I remained thin and underweight and there were those who thought I needed fattening up! Anyway, we were never hungry; we were not allowed to eat between meals so were always ready to enjoy our food.

I remember, when I was aged ten, we had a visit from Uncle Joseph and Auntie Lillie from South Shields. Their daughter, a few years older than me, was a big hefty girl 'wi a face laek a hairst mön'. One evening, Auntie Lillie remarked, "Chrissie had a sixpenny face." I was not at all chuffed, I can tell you. I secretly longed to be big and sturdy like my cousin. I even tried puffing out my cheeks in a vain effort to blow up my face as big as half-a-croon!

I do have a memory of the pupils of East Burrafirth Side School, along with our teacher, being invited to a prize giving at Aith in 1926. It was a sunshiny day. First we got ferried across the narrow creek of the voe at East Burrafirth in a small flat bottom skyiff, from the pier at Hametoon to the Burgans noost. From there we climbed up to the road and walked the three miles to Aith School.

I can remember joining in games down on the flat green sward above the beach, just below the school. I recall going through some of those games of long ago – Nuts in May; Out and In the Window; The Grand Old Duke of York and The Jolly Miller, or it could have been Here We Go Round the Mulberry Bush. It would be interesting to discover whether any of those old-fashioned games are still in vogue today. Somehow I doubt it. Everything has changed, so I expect those games which I remember will have been lost along the way too.

Anyway, we all got prize books. I still have the first one I received for merit and attendance – *Two Little Travellers* by Ray Cunningham. It got read over and over many times and is still worth reading after all these years, in spite of it being in a well-worn condition.

By the time we returned from our jaunt to Aith School it was an ebb tide, which meant we had to walk almost to the head of the voe and make a crossing on foot over huge stepping stones which cross the burn just below the Hoit house. That must have been my first encounter with those ungainly huge rocks – really meant for adults with long legs. I can still recall the feeling of dismay which overcame me. I was more concerned that I might drop my precious book in the burn, than the prospect of slipping between those stepping stones and getting my feet wet. Our teacher solved the problem by suggesting that we take off our shoes and stockings and wade across at a point further out where the burn spread out more across the sand.

Once there came to be a school at Aith, our side school at East Burrafirth somehow came under the control of the Aith head teacher, Mr Willie Laurenson. He used to come once or twice a year to make an inspection of the pupils' progress, etc.

Another gentleman had a job as Attendance Officer. He appeared on a regular basis to inspect the attendance register. I am not certain, but I assume he had power to visit a parent or guardian whose child had been kept off school to help with the croft work or whatever. There were those children too, who had no love of learning from books, who tried to stay home for a day or two. I remember trying that dodge once, but I got quite a ticking off from my elders and felt so bad about being untrue to myself I never tried it a second time. Of course, if a child was really unwell then a certificate of unfitness had to be procured from the doctor. We called it a 'tifficat'.

The attendance officer for Aithsting came from Flawtoon in Clousta. His name was John Tait; a tall dark man, who was easily recognisable as soon as he appeared on the road corners of Scarvataing or Hestataing. If that happened while we were out at playtime, a cry would go up: "Here comes Longatoog!" At that time we were not acquaint with such a tall man. I wondered how it was that he could apparently twist those long thin legs around each other. The East Burrafirth men didn't have legs that were long enough to do a twist! Someone had to ferry him across the voe and he always got a cup of tea at the Hametoon. Besides walking to East Burrafirth and Aith schools, John Tait had to inspect registers at West Burrafirth and Twatt. Maybe he did Sandsound School too, and of course he also visited Clousta School.

Even though our small school at East Burrafirth was indeed a primitive place, even by the standards of the 1920s, it was a happy place. As far as I was aware there was no bullying. Our teacher dealt with us all as one big family.

19
Church

MY father and Auntie Ellen belonged to, or I should say were members of, the Methodist Chapel at Gonfirth in South Delting. From early childhood we all regularly attended meetings there – even though it took an hour to walk across a very awkward, broken-grounded hill. I always found a homeliness at the Chapel of Gonfirth where everyone was very down to earth.

I also attended the Church of Scotland at Aith regularly and about 1936 a few other teenagers joined me in becoming members. At East Burrafirth school there were gospel meetings held by all denominations – except Methodists.

Gonfirth Chapel

Harvest Thanksgivings bring back memories of long ago at the Gonfirth Methodist Chapel, which was built in 1900. The very first thanksgiving service I ever attended would have been around 1922, when I would have been almost at my fifth birthday.

Besides viewing the chapel, decorated in the usual way, for the very first time I was more entranced by the sound of music coming from the organ, which was half hidden by the archway decorated with corn and flowers. Maggie Hunter, with whom I was well acquainted, was the organist; she began playing, and everybody got to their feet to sing the catchy melody of "Bringing in the sheaves".

At home we had a phonograph, with quite a number of cylinder records – mostly of hymns but there were some old songs too. But to hear and see someone actually make music, by moving their fingers over a keyboard and pumping in air to the instrument by pedalling with both feet was a new one on me!

Harvest Thanksgiving certainly had much more meaning all those years ago. Sheaves were actually brought in, tied in bundles and carried on backs well used to bearing burdens. In some places they would have been brought in by horse and cart, but not so at our croft at Slyde where everything depended on muscle power. Nowadays, it is a rarity to see a sheaf of corn. Huge black bags, filled with winter feeding meet the eye, no matter where one looks.

But that long-ago Harvest Thanksgiving was by no means the first time I had been inside the Chapel at Gonfirth, for I was told by my Auntie Ellen that she and my mother had carried me, as an infant of about six months, all the way across the Hill o' Burrafirth to be christened at Gonfirth. With never a peester I had behaved myself, as they had hoped, all through the proceedings. Dat wis a winder!

After the service they had been taken down to Winnaness, to get my nappy changed and my bottle of milk warmed up. Auld Bessie, who by that time was nearing her 90th birthday, held me in her lap, crooning endearments like "Peerie sweet love" all the while. I don't suppose, on that day, that I could have been a heavy burden. There used to be an old adage that a hen in Northmavine seemed as heavy as a goose by the time she had been carried to Lerwick! But of course, when two folk share, the weight is lighter.

The folk from Slyde had all been members of the Methodist Chapel at Gonfirth. My paternal grandmother, Margaret Nicolson, had been born at Quienster, a niece of the John Nicolson who is said to have been the man who first brought Methodism to Shetland. I can't say for sure, but I think meetings were first held at Gonfirth on a fortnightly rota and came within the North Roe circuit, so I guess that's why records show some of my siblings to have been baptised in North Roe. I'm sure if family members had made any journey to North Roe I would have heard about it; I'm almost certain they went no further than Gonfirth for baptisms. Other lay-preachers took the services too.

There always seemed to be an extra homeliness within the chapel at Gonfirth which somehow seemed to be missing at Aith Kirk, where nobody would have turned their heads to look around them, nor even to whisper to each other. Even though I became a member of Aith Church of Scotland while still a teenager, I seemed aware of a sort of warmer atmosphere at Gonfirth. The folk who lived there were more or less middle-aged and elderly people and there was a hamely down-to-earth feeling within its walls. A great deal of chatting and laughing would be exchanged before the service began. Most Sundays a good-going peat fire gave out a splendid heat and on winter evenings the glow from that fire seemed a welcome in itself. Wet coats were often spread out along the edge of the back seats to dry out after a shower of rain had overtaken us on our way there.

On the north end of the chapel there was (and still is) a small living room with a smaller bedroom opening off and a turning stairway leading to an upstairs bedroom. I still have a vivid memory of Auntie Ellen taking me across to the chapel to join one or two women in a general clean-up project. I was about eight years of age. I was given a tin of Mansion polish and a duster or two and set on to give a shine to all the seats, the pulpit and rails, not forgetting the wonderful box of music. I was sent down to Winnaness – The Unseen Stores – for a loaf of bread and I remember getting a sweetie or two from Baabie.

I had a great day tripping up and down the pulpit steps and more so up and down the twisted stair from living room to bedroom. There was a big chest in the upstairs room crammed full of blankets and other bedding. For a time a minister by the name of Mainland, and his wife, dwelt in the rooms there — and a baby boy had been born there around 1912.

Later on I remember Isa Thompson and her brother from Scalloway living in the so-called vestry. Isa was a musician so she played the organ – that seemed to keep the Shetland collie dogs yalkin'. Maybe the sound of music and rough singing voices grated on their ears.

There are many more memories of those hamely folk connected to Gonfirth. I have sometimes met them in my dreams! All so vivid, so that when I awaken from sleep I am filled with pleasure at meeting again in my sub-conscious mind those hamely folk from long ago.

Methodist Chapel, Aith

The roofless walls of the earlier Methodist Chapel still stand and can be seen on the south side of the hill above the Ayres croft. I don't know whether that section of hill had this special name, but that old chapel was referred to as

Lingarö. I assume that place of worship had been built to accommodate the people from Clousta and Noonsbrough, as well as the local Aith folk and those from East Burrafirth, as well those townships on the south edge of Delting parish. I can remember my father telling of quite a few boat loads of people crossing west across Aith Voe to attend that chapel on the hill, but in my time it has always been roofless. Gonfirth Methodist Chapel was built in 1900, so it would seem that the meeting place at Lingarö ceased to be attended after the Church of Scotland at the head of Aith Voe got a footing here.

In the census for 1881 I found a woman, named Margaret Nicolson, aged 52, born in Delting, living in the vestry at Lingarö. Her occupation is down as knitter, but she would also have been the caretaker, so probably lived rent free. Her only payment could have been a roof over her head. No doubt she may well have helped the folk round about, who may have supplied her with milk. She could have had a few hens scratching around on the hill which could have kept her supplied with eggs. Away back in those days, wants were few and folk were contented with little.

I have sometimes wondered why it was that it was the council houses at Bixter which got the name of Lingarö. Why were those houses at Aith not so named? Lingarö is a much nicer name than Whitelaw Road or Wirliegert! – especially seeing Lingarö is a name belonging to Aith and not to Bixter? Maybe I am wrong here for I do not know for certain what the Norse sounding name Lingarö really means.

Missionaries who came to East Burrafirth

East Burrafirth school also served as a place where gospel meetings were held; even after the school closed those meetings continued for a number of years. All denominations came to preach the word of God. Church of Scotland men came from Aith and sometimes from Clousta on a regular fortnightly basis. Then, for a few years during the months of summer, a band of Plymouth Brethren held meetings on Sunday evenings. Mr William Huggins often preached too and later his son, Kenny Huggins. Faith Mission women came as well so we were well steeped in religious schooling as far back as I can remember.

Nannie Tait also kept a Sunday School and when I became a teenager I helped her. Later still, Jeannie Anderson kept a Sunday School going.

Lack of a road did not discourage other denominations coming too, nor did stormy wintry weather deter those who wished to attend. Before a road got laid, those missionaries from Aith had to be transported across the narrow creek of the voe, usually from the noost at Selkieburn over to the Wasthoose small pier, on the north side, in a small rowing boat. On a lovely summer evening it would have been a pleasant enough trip but not so in winter time. Sometimes the young folk from Aith came to these meetings – probably to eye up the 'talent' rather than religious fervour!

When I was a schoolgirl we had to prepare for those meetings, setting out trestles and laying long planks of wood across them to the make seating. All that gear was stored in what was called 'Da Black End', along with peats for the school fire, and other things besides.

Two old-fashioned paraffin-filled hanging lamps were trimmed and their glasses cleaned. All those years ago there was no organ, so someone had to raise da singing. Usually a woman took on the job of being precentor – I remember both Lizzie Tait from da Punds and Beenie Eunson from da Lea.

It would be impossible to write down all I can remember concerning all those meetings we faithfully attended. Each group had their own favourite hymns. I can recall the words of most of them and see in my mind's eye all those folk who went to those meetings of long ago. I can even recall the clothes they wore!

Mr Drife

The Aith Church of Scotland was built sometime about 1910 and opened in 1911. The manse got built a few years later. I have been told that the first missionary to come was a man whose surname was Drife. Apparently, he got accommodation beside Mr and Mrs William Tait at North Braewick. It may have been after he got married that he lived at Sunnybank, near the shop. A child was born there. I am not certain if they would have been the very first inmates of the newly built manse.

Mr Charleston

Next, I think, came Mr Charleston; he was unmarried. I know he was here in 1922 but don't know when he arrived or left. I was too young to remember what he looked like, though I can recall being taken to my first gospel meeting in the small schoolroom at East Burrafirth aged about three, when Mr Charleston was the preacher. He must have been giving a short talk to the children which went over my head, figuratively and literally, I being too young to understand the story. Anyway, young Johnny from Selkieburn, a boy aged about 10, held up his hand, and answered the question by saying "Jesus". I can still remember becoming quite alert on hearing this new word which I thought was cheese. Now, in those far away times, cheese was indeed a rare commodity, though I had tasted it once or twice and loved its flavour. I was indeed most disappointed when I realised there was no cheese forthcoming! Of such are the memories of early childhood.

Mr Bennie

Mr Hugh Bennie arrived with his wife about 1925 or 26, and left in 1930. They had no family but did quite a lot of visiting among all the houses in the district. I can well remember them coming to our house at Slyde for their tea. A white tablecloth was spread and the one and only good tea-set taken out! Whether they got boiled eggs or not I don't recall for we children had our meal at a small table at the other side of the but-end.

Mr Wyse

Mr Alexander Wyse came next. He was responsible for getting an organ installed in the East Burrafirth schoolroom in 1931. He was also keen that Nancy Tait from Wasthoose and I should learn to play that instrument, and even offered to give us music lessons at the manse. I can remember we went along a few times to have a go at the piano. I am sorry to say it petered out – mainly because we had no organ at home. We had no money to buy such a thing, and besides, our elders did not encourage us wasting our time on having music lessons. "Du'll niver hae time tae sit an' waste on playin an organ. Du haes far mair need ta be makkin dee sock," they said.

I still remember being at the Holm and seeing two men rowing a boat from Aith, carrying a most unusual load – an organ precariously balanced in the boat, held on by Mr Wyse. I expect men from around the Wasthoose and Hametoon would have helped carry the organ up to the old school. Betty Tait died the week after the organ arrived so one of the first times it was played there was at her funeral, when they sang "Forever with the Lord".

Mr Graham

After Mr and Mrs Wyse moved away, I think William Graham arrived. He was missionary in Aith for quite a number of years, from about 1937 until 1945. He was a bachelor who brought his mother along as housekeeper. They kept a parrot, which perched along the back and arms of a high basket chair; more than likely it had free range all over the kitchen, but I was only there two or three times. His mother had a bread knife with a tartan handle so she got the nickname of "tartan tully".

William Graham was not really a robust man – somewhat stiff and ungainly in his movements. Besides that his eyesight was impaired so the trip to East Burrafirth must have been an ordeal. He walked to Selkieburn where Jeemie Sandison (senior) from Hestataing, who was an elder in the Aith Kirk, would meet him and take him down to the pier, where a boat awaited to transport them across. He had to be helped into the boat and, on reaching the other side, would have been more or less man-handled out of the boat and onto dry land – all depending on the state of the tide.

Even after the trachle of the boat crossing he still had an uphill walk over uneven ground to cover and a small burn to cross, which boasted only a couple of stepping stones. Many a time Frankie Tait and another youth helped in getting Willie Graham across, lifting him bodily over the rough places: "Come on, old fellow, we'll gyit you safely dere." He usually entered the meeting place puffin' an' blowin' after his exertions.

Of course, once the road came the boat journey was abandoned and he walked right around the head of the voe, often accompanied by John Hunter from Annesville, each of them armed with bright torches. Coming past da Punds Puddle you could have been misled in thinking a car might be on its way, except for the slower speed! They had much need of those torches, for once they reached the grind at the top of the Hametoon road, they still had a nasty broo at Da Stibbly to descend, then to cross a small streamlet which ran as an overflow from the well. For two men, both with impaired eyesight, it must indeed have been hazardous. I assume someone may have met them and guided them safely into the haven of the old schoolroom. One thing Mr Graham could do was sing and play the organ, filling the small room with melody.

Right: Circa 1935: at the door of what was then
the East Burrafirth school. Back, left to right:
Jeemie Sandison (Hestataing), Nannie Tait
(Hametoon), Mr Graham (missionary). Front:
Laura Tait and Maggie Tait – Nannie's nieces.

Sometimes, when there was no moon-light, the meetings were held at the Selkie-burn house. Then we from the north side of the Voe made the journey across.

Even after all those years, memories of long past times often invade my subconscious mind – especially in that twilight zone, before deep sleep takes over. I can still hear echoes of voices singing and of those earnest preachers, giving out a message of faith and hope which has been a stay and comfort all through life. Now they have all passed to an altitude sweeter, yet are remembered by what they have done.

Mr Smith

Mr and Mrs Smith came around 1946 and were here a few years before moving to Cunningsburgh or Whiteness. They had two adopted children.

Mr Wallace

Sometime around 1951 or early 1952, Mr Wallace came. He had a German wife who had three sons from a previous marriage. I don't think they could have been here for very long.

Mr Nicol

Alexander Nicol came to Aith manse along with his wife, Bella, and daughter, Evelyn. They stayed for 12 years. Mr Nicol preached his farewell service on 19th September, 1965. He and his wife both came from the Dundee area and on leaving Aith they went to Gourdon, a small fishing town on the east coast of Kincardineshire. I think it could have been Mr Nicol who held the last meetings in East Burrafirth school in the 1960s. Their daughter Evelyn still keeps in contact and visits old school friends made while living in Aith Manse.

20

Trips Away from Home

Visits to Lerwick

My first visit to Lerwick was in July 1928, when I was ten years old. My Auntie Ellen and I had gone to visit Auntie Mimie at Sandsound. From there we had a day at Lerwick. I don't think either of my aunts did any shopping. I remember a visit to cousins, a gravestone for their sister (my mother) being chosen, and a trip to Ramsay the photographer, to have the photograph taken.

I think my next trip to Lerwick was when I was about 14, in 1932. We must have had a telegram to say that my brother Johnnie was coming home on the steamer from Aberdeen, so Auntie Ellen decided she and I would go to meet him. We went by boat to Scarvataing then walked to the Voehead – John o' da Voehead was sent to the Ayres to hire the car to take us to meet the steamer, which was due in Lerwick about 6am. We left Aith about midnight – I don't remember what time we reached the pier in Lerwick but do recall we had a long, long time to wait for the steamer. I have a studio photo of me with Johnnie, but I'm not sure if we made another

The author – first trip to Lerwick.

91

trip to Lerwick while he was home, or if we went to the photographer before we left Lerwick.

Each village had at least one or two men who owned vehicles which were the local hire cars. There were no restrictions on passenger numbers so as many people as needed to squashed into the cars. For anyone making a long journey it could be quite uncomfortable and they'd need to stretch their legs whenever the vehicle stopped. To hire one of these taxis either the hirer or a messenger cycled or walked to their house to make the arrangements.

Aith Regatta

In 1922 I went to Aith Regatta for the first time. We – Mimie, John Robert, Liza and I – were rowed from Slyde to the Scarvataing noost. We then walked to Pirliegert (North Pund) where I remember Willie, who'd been born the previous November, was sitting on his mother's knee. I hadn't seen many babies and was taken with his 'aafil head o' hair' – very fair and curly.

Later we walked up to Gudataing, but the weather deteriorated so much that sailing was postponed. We went into the old store which was packed with

Starting a race at Aith regatta.

people escaping the rain. A navy ship, *Thunderer*, lay in the Bight o' Braewick for what seemed like most of the summer. When the weather was still, or the wind blowing from the west, we could hear the bugles blowing – that frightened me, and drove the Slyde kye haywire so Auntie Ellen kept them in the byre till reveille was over. At the regatta some of the uniformed crew were ashore and sheltered in the store too – I remember one of them lifting me up so I could see what was going on. I suppose I'd never seen so many people before, as people came from a wide area of Shetland to attend the regatta.

The weather was too windy and wet for us to travel home so we stayed in Lochside all night. I have no doubt seventeen-year-old Liza would have been at the dance in the store.

Visits to Burra

Maggie from the Hametoon had met her husband, John Christie from Burra, when she went to the (herring) gutting. After she married in 1914, she lived in Burra with John, his mother and sister. In 1936 I went on a visit to Auntie Meggie and Baabie at Scalloway when Maggie, who'd come to Scalloway to do some shopping, also came visiting. Seeing me there, she immediately invited me to return to Burra with her, so off I went for about a week – quite an adventure getting to see another part of Shetland. A lifelong friendship with Laura Christie from Houss started then.

I went to see Maggie quite a few times after that, usually spending a few nights in Scalloway before and after visiting Burra. Sometimes Babsy would be with me, for she had met a young Jamieson fellow whose attentions she enjoyed. He was at the herring fishing and, in June 1937, his boat came to the pier at Voe. He had his bicycle with him so arrived at the Hametoon one day to see Babsy – they wrote to each other so she may have known to expect him. When it came time to return to his boat, Babsy followed him to the top of the Muckle Knowe, telling him she hoped he had good brakes. Unfortunately, he came to grief going down towards Voe – where the road is very steep, and at that time uneven and untarred – at Kringrigyill, where his body was later found lying at the side of the burn. A good while after this accident I was with Babsy next time she visited Burra, when we went with Maggie to visit the Jamieson family. Babsy probably appreciated the company on what would have been a difficult visit for her to make.

21
Long Ago at Christmas

ALTHOUGH Foula may be the only place in Shetland nowadays where Christmas is still held by the old style on 6th January, I can remember when most other country districts did the same. I think East Burrafirth changed over to the 25th December in the mid-1920s, though many other places still held on to the 5th or 6th of January.

My very first memories of our Christmas are of having a quiet sense of contentment after a week or so of subdued excitement, wondering whether Santa Claus would really come. I had never even seen a picture of that rosy cheeked old man, for I don't remember Christmas Cards arriving or being sent in the 1920s – not in our house anyway.

Sometimes a reference might have been made to this obscure someone who, to my childish ears, sounded like a fellow named Saandy Gless! He, of course, existed only in my imagination – he still does! To be honest, this name Saandy Gless wasn't attractive to me at all, for I disliked the feel of sand on my hands – and glass covered with sand was most repulsive. It made water run among my teeth!

I remember that from about 1922-23 we had a but-bed. It was, I suppose, a sort of box-bed though not quite, because instead of drawing doors there were floral curtains which I always pulled together when I undressed and donned my nightgown. I needed always to leave a gap in those curtains so I could see my elders sitting around the stove; the women folk always knitting, and the men with their noses in a book. About this time all-over Fair Isle patterned jumpers came into high fashion. Miss Adie of Voe got huge orders and apparently good prices were paid. I don't expect the knitters got ready cash – but I am not certain of that. While I lay in our but-bed trying to stay awake, though more than likely half-asleep, I would always see a big all-over jumper stretched upon a wooden frame hanging up near the stove so as to be all ready for market, maybe next morning.

Anyway, in our house there were at that time three women knitting away every spare moment – my Auntie Ellen, my sister Liza and sister-in-law Mimie. That added quite a bit to the family budget.

Quite early on a December morning one of those three would set out for Voe with the big shopping basket packed with hosiery. They knew lots of kind folk around Voe so would call along one of them for a rest, a cup of tea and to exchange news, before setting off for home again with a heavy basket now full of shopping. Someone always set off to meet whoever had been to Voe so as to relieve her of her load.

My father would always ask, "Did you see Saandy wi da claw ony whaar aroond da Muckle Knowe?"

"Yis, yis," was always the answer. My nephew John Robert (about three years my junior), and I, would then discuss between ourselves what we had heard and came to the conclusion that Saandy Gless was getting nearer.

At last Christmas came and we got our stockings hung up on each side of the but mantelpiece. When bedtime came it was hard to get to sleep. The unsteady candle flame cast eerie shadows in the corners of my bedroom upstairs, and if a strong wind was blowing it tended to make a dunderin' noise in the chimney. I was so very scared, not knowing who or what might appear, so I took the blankets over my head and lay until I could scarcely breath, until forced to lift a corner to let in some air.   Eventually I fell asleep, until John Robert came along banging and shouting, "Chrissie, du'll hae ta rise."

Goodness knows what time it would have been for it was pitch dark. With trembling hands I got the candle lit, after crawling out of bed past my aunt – who pretended to be asleep. Next we got my sister Maggie up too. We needed someone to get the fire going and tea made. Maggie was four years my senior so she knew all about Saandy Gless though she never let on she knew.

I don't think anything in later life could ever compare to the thrill we felt on those cold mornings of long ago, on surveying those long black stockings. The toys, and my small doll which had been tied outside the stocking (she seemed to be smiling at me), wouldn't impress today's youngsters but we were enchanted and thought they were super. Among the bits and pieces there was always a net Santa sock in which there was a tootie horn made of cardboard with a whistle affair on the end.

Once, I remember John Robert getting a tin tootie horn. We decided to let everybody else in our house know that Saandy Gless had actually been so we each took a candle and our horn and called along all those beds. We were so excited and we were making some din. We got on all right until we entered the boys' room, some of whom perhaps had only just got to bed (after a night on the tiles) We shouted, "Happy Christmas," and blew our horns with mighty breath. Peter took his blankets over his head but we lifted the edge of his quilt and gave another blast. "Pit oot dat light at wanse; get oot o' here an' mak less noise." I daresay it would have been the skruffling of the older boys trying to be quiet as they got into bed that had awakened John Robert in the first place.

We hurried downstairs where Maggie had let her cat in. She had the fire going and a pot of tea as well as glasses of ginger cordials and slices of cake. By and by the grown-ups came downstairs (except for those who perhaps had been making merry on Christmas Eve). My father would bring down his bottle of whisky and one of port wine, as well as green ginger for us children.

I did have faith that Santa would come 'doon da lum' until I was about seven years old, by which time, another girl, three years older than me, let me into the secret. She told me how she and her older brother had made a search underneath their parents' bed and thereby managed to prove something. Of course, I never let on what I discovered, for once one knew – or if parents knew that a child knew – then clods of peat or boiled mutton bones, besides other useless odds and ends, might be found in a stocking.

Coming near Christmas I spent quite some time searching under beds for this cache, but never was successful in discovering anything; though I imagine I would have got a fair amount of dust for I searched under a few beds. On thinking back over all those years, that box of surprises may well have been hidden in the barn or among sheaves of cattle fodder, or in some dark corner where they knew muggins would have been too scared to approach. But somehow, I thought it must be under somebody's bed.

In our home at Slyde, in the days I write about, I remember eight beds. Upstairs (abune but), which was the boys' room, there were three beds – two built-in wooden beds joined to each other filled the length of the room (opposite the skylight) with another along the partition. My father's bed was in what was called 'da cubicle', on the other side of the partition from the boys' room. On the right hand side of the stairs there were two beds, one of which I slept in along with my Auntie Ellen. Downstairs, ben da hoose, there were another two beds, standing end to end along the back waa. So with all those beds I had any amount of hunting ground!

One other memory about Christmas was that our lunch on Boxing Day was always either salt herring or dried salt fish and tatties! Supposedly 'ta settle wir stamicks' to counteract having eaten too many sweet things at Christmas.

22

Those Lights of Yesterday

THERE are so many outside lights nowadays that one can at times feel blinded and confused by the glare. Yet I can't help trying to recall how it actually was years ago – before electricity came along.

Paraffin and candles

The old paraffin lamps shed only a soft glow which would not have penetrated the outside darkness of a winter night. I daresay, that with a clear sky and a full moon, it would have been much brighter outside than in.

I have no recollection of the colly lamp which burned fish oil, though I understand there were still a few being used in byres early on last century. My earliest memory is of hanging paraffin oil lamps of the kind you can see in any of our museums. Those lamps were hung from a beam or joist in the but-end. Ben da hoose there was a standing lamp and upstairs in our house there seemed always to be a lamp standing on the mantelpiece, but candles were very much in use elsewhere.

When I was very young we had a but-bed. What a lovely place that was – so cosy and warm and bright. But after my grandmother died, in early spring 1924, a change took place. It was decided to demolish the but-bed and use the space, along with a few feet taken from the living room, to make a small closet under the stairs. A window on the back of the house was divided so that daylight could also enter the closet, which became a handy place to hang wearing jackets and to store boots. But when darkness fell we children lit a candle and lived in our own small world of make-believe – not at all such a bad place, when compared to the realities of life!

Now I had to sleep upstairs with my Auntie Ellen in the south room, the cause and root of all those imaginary fears which were to take possession of me on reaching the head of the stairs. With only a candle in my trembling hand, nasty things would enter my mind. I would be reminded of those dreadful words often whispered in my ear: "Green eyes i da glory-höl. Did du see dem?" Yes, I had, and I was still too young to understand that those eyes really belonged to Polly, our old cat, and that it was actually reflected light which made her eyes glow green in the darkness. The glory-hole held those spinning wheels and rowers and teased wool – a fine cosy place for a cat to sleep, but a place of terror for a scared peerie lass. The memory of this has stayed so vividly with me that it led to my first published poem in 1981 "Cats een i da dark", a poem about my life and fears as a peerie lass trying to get up and down da stairs. (Appendix 14)

Aladdin lamps

After the hanging lamp, the Aladdin lamp came along. What a lovely white light it shed around the but-end. The only snag was that when the round wick had not been properly cleaned, or if the merest speck of crust had been left on the wick, it tended to make a black patch on the fragile mantle. Then the wick had to be turned down until the black patch wore off and for the rest of the evening the light had to be kept lower.

I think Aladdin lamps came into being in the late 1920s.

Tilleys

Tilleys were next – maybe not until the end of the 1930s, but I can't really remember. Until folk got used to getting the vaporiser properly heated by a 'moose' soaked in methylated spirit and set alight for that purpose, many an impatient fellow turned on the paraffin too soon so that it flared up with a whoosh, almost singeing his eyebrows. There were also those who were scared of the tilley and always had to get someone to light it for them – until I suppose they did get the hang of the thing. Very soon most folk learned how a tilley lamp should be lit and all was well.

All those lamps had to be kept clean and usually from August, all through the winter, they had to be filled with paraffin while wicks had to be evened up, mantles fitted, etc., etc. It was a chore. But until the early 1950s that was how it was – before we actually got electric power.

Early text messages

A vivid memory to do with flashing lights dates from 1922 while my grandmother was still alive. She slept upstairs in the sooth room. Her bed (hung about with curtains to shield her from draughts) stood in a corner opposite the fire, which was always kept on and rested at nights (especially during the winter months).

My sister Liza and her chum, Mootie Tait from da Hametoon, both of the same age, had boy friends from Aith – from around the Gerts and Uphoose or around da Biggans area, all houses which were quite visible to each other in daylight. More than likely there was a pre-arranged plan to make contact with each other by Morse code!

I can see them yet in my mind's eye. At that time our house had what was called stormy windows upstairs – partly in the wall and partly in the roof, the deep sill on the inside was about a foot above floor level. Mootie was in the floor of the window on her knees, with a copy of Manson's *Almanac* in which there was a chart of the Morse alphabet. She also had a writing pad and pencil and a blinky to see what she was trying to decipher. Liza knelt on the floor with her elbows in the window recess. The lower sash of the window was raised as far as it could go. In her hand she also had a blinky. It was she who took and sent those messages to and from those fellow-me-lads across the water. Maybe this was the beginnings of text messaging that is so popular with courting couples today?

I don't know for sure, but I think Liza had got the idea from our eldest brothers who were all seamen. It was common for one of them to spend a while in the porch door on a clear winter evening exchanging news across the water. All the men were seamen in those days so learning the Morse code would have been part of their lives. I imagine the time for calling would have been pre-arranged. Anyone who could read Morse code could have got the messages, and there was no way to be certain of who was replying to them!

Anyway, the teenage lasses certainly made contact and got information concerning box-socials and dances up in da Nort Store o' Gudataing. All this took place before a public hall was opened in Aith.

Two lasses wasting their time lying in the window did not go down very well with Auntie Ellen: "Better hed you been makkin your socks," or "Shut dat window, you're lettin a cowld wind inta grandmidder's room," etc.

I can tell you I was not really welcome, standing there with my ears alert, yet at the same time peering into all the shadowy corners. They were scared I might disclose some of their messages sent and received. But I was too scared to go downstairs by myself for fear I might meet the owner of those big green eyes.

Electric light

The west side of Aith and around the head of the voe as far as the Voehead got electricity maybe a year or so before we did at Hestataing and the rest of East Burrafirth. I was a bit envious of those so near who could have a light and heat by merely pressing a switch while we were still 'virgin wi paraffin lamps'.

Jeemie had wired up our house at Hestataing before going to the whaling at South Georgia. Such was our delight to have at last got electricity that a cable was sent saying "Power switched on today. Everybody happy!" And so we were.

All those things are only memories to us who have reached the sunset years. We would not feel fit for lots of those chores of long ago but then, of course, where there was a houseful of folk each had, or was expected to have, his special jobs to do. Many hands made light work. While somebody's hands were busy filling those paraffin lamps others were doing something else. So the old traditional way of life had its advantages and as I look back there are many good things to be remembered.

23

Scarlet Fever

IN April 1934 there was an outbreak of scarlet fever at the Hametoon – that was not an uncommon occurrence in those far back days. Sometimes it could creep in among a young family without anyone having a clue as to where it had come from.

This particular outbreak came in with Barbara Tait (eldest of Betty o' da Hametoon's family), who had been attending the School for the Blind in Edinburgh since early 1933. It appears there had been an outbreak of scarlet fever among some of the children there. When Barbara came home for Easter, 1934, she must have been at the contagious stage, for not long afterwards the other children began to develop sore, inflamed throats and high fever, with a red rash soon to follow.

After the doctor had confirmed it to be all the symptoms of scarlet fever the whole household of four adults and six children were under quarantine, which meant it was well into the month of June before they were free to mix with other people – and only after the whole house had been fumigated by the Sanitary Inspector. Every stitch of clothes and all bedding had to be washed. Scarlet fever was a dreaded disease and children could often develop ear infections etc.

I am not certain, but I think Babsy o' da Hametoon escaped the first onslaught of that disease though probably she got it later. Although there was a Fever Hospital at Lerwick at that time, it would have been impossible for a whole family to be admitted at once.

Help from Muckle Roe

Outside help was needed, and could only be found from someone who'd already had the disease. It happened that a Johnson family then living at South

Scord, Muckle Roe, met the requirements. Jeemie Tait from Biggans in Aith set off in his small motor boat to find out whether one of the Johnson lasses could possibly come to help out the stricken family at Hametoon. Anyway, it was Ina Johnson who came to help look after the cows, hens etc., besides all the other everyday chores and attending to the sick.

Here, I would need to explain that over the years before the 1930s there was a great coming and going between the South Scord lasses and the Tait lasses from East Burrafirth. I can remember many visits being exchanged, not only with the family at South Scord, but also with Maggie and Agnes Johnson at The Dyke, Brae. Those Johnsons at Muckle Roe and at The Dyke were related to the Taits of Hametoon. On those visits they always took with them a supply of yarn to keep them knitting which in those days was often their only means of livelihood.

Helping the neighbours

That April, Lollie, who was a seaman, had just returned to Britain from a trip at sea. A telegram was sent to let him know how circumstances were at home. He had little option but to pack his bag and make for East Burrafirth. He, of course, had to keep a wide berth of his own home so he came to Slyde, where he got his meals and a bed for the night.

Neighbours gathered together in an effort to get all the voar work done. A lot of the Hametoon croft could be turned by the plough and I think it was my brother Robbie who was ploughman. One other memory springs into my mind at this stage. One morning, when Lollie and Robbie went to bring the mares out of the lambhouse at Slyde, where they had been housed overnight, they got quite a shock to discover that one of them had produced a foal! Not knowing that Queenie had been pregnant they'd had her yoked to a plough throughout her pregnancy. She must have been a mare of stamina and in good condition. I can't remember whether they got another pony to take her place, but they must have.

Anyway, that spring we actually did three voars. My brother Robbie had taken over the croft of Quienster in 1932. That was how ponies came in on our scene. Our croft at Slyde was a very heavy working place and no plough was set in there until 1935 when Queenie's foal, by then a gelding named Charlie, was thought fit enough to be yoked with his mother to pull a plough.

So, besides all the barrow and spade work on our own croft, some ground was also cultivated at Quienster and on top of that there was all the voar work at Hametoon. No wonder I have memories of crawling to bed every night fairly dead-beat. We still had no road to make things easier but I was young and strong at that time and we always had any amount of good wholesome food.

Peter trying his hand at a straight furrow at Quienster.

24

Caain da Marrofield Sheep – 1936

THE subject for this chapter came out of the blue! I had a vivid dream: I was taken back in time to when I was a teenager again! I was back in the old house at Slyde: there was a knocking on the partition, someone was shouting, "Du'll need to rise at wanse! We're goin' tae da Marrofield sheep in an hour's time."

I awoke with a start, glad to realise it had only been a dream, though I do often wish I had a fraction of the energy I had all those years ago. Memories came flooding back.

In those days Slyde was a house of young folk so after a substantial breakfast of bacon and egg we were ready for off: at least four of us, most likely my father, plus whichever of my brothers was home, or our cousin Peter, my nephew John Robert, and me, along with two dogs.

The other owners of those sheep at Marrofield were the Taits from the Haa in East Burrafirth – a very depleted household at the time I am writing about. Jeemie Tait would have been into his sixties and pretty well crippled with arthritis. His sister Katie was worse than he was (I don't ever remember seeing her any further than the doorstep). A niece lived with them, Eppie Leask. She had a great interest in her sheep so it was she who came to caa. She always had two huge black dogs (Glen and Mark) and she always seemed to be shouting at one or the other, "Go hom!" Not that she really meant it, but maybe it was her method of keeping control?

It was a long trek before we eventually reached our target – up hill and down dale for miles. The foot of Marrofield was really just up the valley from Setter at Voe. After ascending Da East Hill o' Burrafirth we had to tackle Da Dubbs, jumping from broo to broo to keep out of boggy bits. Then an upland incline past the south end of Brettifield (which is a very steep hill, on its west side). On we went until we came in sight of the loch of Marrofield – always referred to as Marlswater. Still further – the trek seemed endless. Those who had dogs to control went furthest – right down to the long deserted croft of Marrofield. We younger ones were left at strategic points above the loch.

That particular morning the sun was shining and bright but with a cool south-east wind. I soon began to feel really cold and stood hopping from leg to leg in an effort to keep warm, ever straining eyes and ears for the approach of the vanguard! There's little need to be writing about all the hassle of a big sheep drive. What I remember most is Eppie Leask's high-pitched shrill voice shouting to me, "Run, Christina, run!" I don't know how it was she always referred to me as Christina but on sheep caains it kept ringing in my ears and it annoyed me. Like the fool I was, I ran, maybe more to get warmed up than in any hope of turning a strong Marrofield hog, for even a strong sheepdog was hard put to head him back to the rest of the milling flock.

Those who had been wearing jackets or cardigans at the outset began to take them off and wrap them around their heads (like wings) in an effort to keep the sheep on the move, with much shouting at disobedient dogs, the waving of scarves and for ever Eppie's voice, wavering at high pitch, "Go hom! Go hom!"

Getting them over Da Dubbs was quite a trachle – no way must they be allowed to get into two separate lots, or the battle would have been lost. Then up the back of the East Hill and down towards the burn. By this time Jeemie Tait from the Haa, and my sister-in-law Mimie would be standing out a good bit from the crö grind. Sometimes Mootie Tait from the Hametoon would come to help caa those Marrofield sheep. She had a red-coloured dog named Spy, so quite a few girns were exchanged between him and his neighbours from the Haa, no doubt making up his mind to have a proper 'set tü' wi Don and Spot from Slyde. Mootie, aye one to have a fun, would say to Eppie, "See du, dere's da sheep owners waitin' fir da shepherds ta bring hame da oo an da mutton." That made Eppie see red, and a wild screeching would be carried along on the light breeze. The noise from the flock prevented either Jeemie or Mimie from hearing Eppie's abusive statements, but Mootie and the others got it all. We had to laugh!

Well, the fun really began as we approached the daek. A bit of netting wire stretched out from the doorway of the crö wasn't really any deterrent to big, strong, wild hogs so someone stood by with two dogs to round them up. Often a dog fight broke out and everyone got excited, with much shouting, even though their tongues hung out with thirst and they longed to sit down for a rest.

Eventually the sheep would be safely in the crö and we could have a short rest before the work of getting their fleeces off began. No doubt ram lambs were sorted then – no special tools; just a sharp knife or teeth.

I don't know if it was this time, or another year, when I got badly sunburnt. By the time we'd got the sheep in and roo'd them my arms, face and the back of my neck were quite sore. Once home, against Auntie Ellen's advice, I dabbed at the sunburn with peroxide – I never did that again.

The first sheep dip I heard about was a thick paste which was mixed with hot water before being further diluted with cold water then dabbed on strategic parts of the sheep. I remember something called Stockholm Tar (derived from fir trees so it had a lovely smell) which was mixed with greth (urine) and dripped onto the sheep. Later, an old boat was set at an angle to contain the dip mixture in one end of the boat. The sheep were then dunked into the dip and lifted across the tafts to the higher end where they were held till the surplus dip dripped off – it needed several strong hands to make this work.

25
Finances

I DARESAY our family in the 1920s onwards may have been better off than some others – not that many in Shetland were wealthy. Ten shillings could buy a basket of messages in 1925. The hosiery knitted by the grown up females in our house was bartered to pay for the shop goods, but my father's purse was taken to the shop too, so if the hosiery wasn't enough to square up the goods purchased then there was always some cash.

My brothers Tom and Davie had had life insurance when they died. In November 1929, a car was hired to take Robbie, Maggie and me to Voe, where we deposited our share of the insurance money into some kind of a savings account. I think this put me off any interest in money for the rest of my life, as it had such unpleasant associations. Even though I didn't have much money that account was untouched for years, until it was eventually used to help buy a car a good while after I was married.

I remember Nannie writing to Faider after Tom's death to say that, while still at sea, Tom had sent her some money to buy things for the wedding. I can still remember the smell of her scented writing paper. She wanted to give this money to Faider; he wrote back telling her it had been a gift to her so was hers to keep.

Another time I recall being given half a crown to offer Nannie towards the cost of sharing a car hire to see Dr Bowie at Parkhall. I couldn't bear to touch the coin in my pocket so was on the way home when I remembered that I hadn't given it to Nannie but couldn't go home with it. Between the Wasthoose and Slyde grinds I threw it as far as I could. Two or three nights later Mimie and Robbie were on their way home when they saw it glinting in their torchlight. They were very surprised that someone would have lost it without either saying so or searching till they found it. There was much speculation over this for many days with each visitor being questioned. I never did tell them the truth, but I did tell Nannie many years later.

Money was very scarce in the 1930s, right up until the beginning of World War Two. The first airstrip at Scatsta was built in the early years of the war so quite a number of middle-aged merchant seamen and crofting men got well paid jobs connected with that project. It was a chance to improve houses etc.

Gradually, the old ways of dellin' and ploughing with horses gave way to small tractors. Even so, women didn't sit and twiddle 'dir tooms'. Better prices for Shetland hosiery were an incentive to coin in money, especially for those who had a natural attraction for gathering cash. On thinking back, I certainly wasn't one of those but we managed. Always being a dreamer, I spent many hours doing things to help other folk with crofting jobs or working peats (unpaid work); I don't have any regrets concerning that. We never were in debt and always kept our heads above water.

26
Work

BEFORE I got married, I had a job in Clark and Company's shop in Aith. This was a thriving business with the shop and a substantial hosiery (knitwear) business. I don't know how many people were employed by the business but

1900: Gudataing, Aith – site of the first shop in Aith.

there were knitters, scourers, dyers, buyers, clerks and dispatchers, as well as those working in the shop. The trade mark for their hosiery was a large C with a drawing of a lark in the centre. Those bringing hosiery to sell went to the buyer's office where they were given a line (credit note) for the shop. No money changed hands and the line was exchanged for goods in the shop. One way of ensuring customer loyalty!

I fairly enjoyed working in the shop; meeting all those people who came for goods. I had to lodge nearby, at Lochside, as it would have been impossible for me to cycle home every night and back again the next morning. I got home on Wednesdays after 1pm, when the shop closed for the afternoon. On Saturdays the shop stayed open until 8pm, so it was late before I reached Slyde. I think the shop was open 9am to 7pm – but never on a Sunday. I usually went back to my digs on the Sunday evening. Wages were low; fifteen shillings a week.

I was called up for wartime service and was interviewed in Lerwick but, as my father had by then turned 70 and the other men of the household were already contributing to the war effort, I was needed to help on the croft. I always had this feeling that I owed a debt to my father and aunt at home so during the summer I was home more often helping with the croft work and the curing of peats – not only our own peats but for many of the neighbours as well.

Section 4

Shopping

27

Shopping in Voe

I HAVE a vague memory of a motor-powered launch from Adie's shop at Voe being used for delivering bread and perhaps other items. I never knew whether this run took place on a weekly or fortnightly basis or was the transaction done according to the favourable mood of our weathermen. I somehow think the men on the Voe launch could have been delivering bread and biscuits from the bakeshop and perhaps paraffin oil to the shop at Aith and to the much smaller one at Selkieburn.

I can recall accompanying Mimie, my sister-in-law, to the Voe shop. We set out fairly early and walked partly across the hill to Gonfirth where we gained the road to Voe, a distance totalling about six to seven miles. Mimie had a basket of hosiery for sale and got groceries to fill the basket in exchange. Mimie, before marriage, had been a housemaid and assistant cook to the Adie family at Voe House, so after her business at the shop was over we proceeded up there and had eats in the kitchen. No way would a peerie gluffed-laek lass ever be allowed to venture further!

Anyway, it came time to get back on board the launch which took us back home. I think they put off goods at some of the houses on the way – Houbanster, etc. The boatmen let us off on a klett named Da White Craig. The water is quite deep there, even at an ebb tide. Some of our men folk, who I daresay had been watching for the launch, came down to help my short legs and a heavy basket safely on to dry land. Lots of childhood memories tend to fade away but that experience remains vivid.

Christie, Katie and Thomasina's shopping trip to Voe

I do remember hearing of one time when Christie Nicolson from Quienster, along with his sister Katie, and Thomasina Balfour from Houbanster, had been on a shopping trip to Voe. They had been quite some time in the shop waiting their turn to be served. While Katie and Thomasina had been getting messages, Christie and other cronies had been 'sniffin da cork'! So he wasn't feeling that bright, though filled with bravado, when at last it was time to head home.

Thomasina, apparently, was at the helm, leaving Christie to attend to hoisting the sail and shifting the tack-hooks. All went well, and they got alongside the small pier at Houbanster where Thomasina's gear was unloaded. Katie Nicolson was not really a boat woman, so Thomasina offered to stay until they were safely at the Quienster noost. Katie was all for it, as by then Christie seemed half-asleep. But he leapt up. No way was he going to trust his boat to someone else! So off they set without Thomasina. I don't know whether Katie or Christie was steering, but it was near ebb tide and somehow they got grounded on Da Stens o' da Millburn which stood out of the water at low tide. The distance between Houbanster and Quienster noost is only a short one and if the wind was northerly they maybe never got a sail up at all, but they drifted along the shore. So there they were, awaiting the rising tide to float them off. Christie took the opportunity to have a nap in the 'efter stammerin' while I imagine poor Katie would have been sitting on a taft on tenterhooks!

Shortly afterwards, Thomasina noticed their plight and ran as fast as she could to help. Others ran from Ladie and Millburn but they all had to wait for the turn of the tide. At first they thought Christie had fallen overboard and perhaps lost his life but Katie gave a shout to let them know that the skipper was having a kip. More than likely he would have had a rude awakening! Luckily, that bit of shore line is a very sheltered spot as Papa Little shields it from the rougher seas of St Magnus Bay and the full force of the Atlantic which feeds it.

I understand it was common for the men folk in charge of a sailing boat to have too much to drink by the time three or four women had waited their turn in the shop. Perhaps bad tempers arose and often the boys and women had to get the boat and all the goods home as best they could under oars instead of sail.

28

Aith Shop

SOON after Edmund Fraser purchased the Vementry estate, plans went ahead to build a house and start a shop. A shop at Gudataing was a welcome asset to Aith and the surrounding district, even though there was no road which meant the sea was still the main highway. Aithsting had been voted a dry area, unlike Delting, so had no permission to sell whisky, etc. Women doing their shopping at Aith could have easy minds on that score and knew they'd not come out from the shop to discover the man in charge of the boat had become pretty well oiled!

Tammie Anderson from Aithsness set up the first shop in 1905; his nephew Andrew Tait from Greenmeadow was the first shop assistant, I've been told. A small free-standing post office came into being around 1912. Big stores were built too, but I do not know exactly when. About this time another house of similar design was built on to the back of Gudataing. I do not know anything about when Sunnybank got erected but have been told that before Aith Manse was built the first missionary lived there, so it must have been sometime before 1920.

After the boating accident in 1904, Tammie Anderson became factor for the Vementry Estate, whose ownership was transferred to Miss Evelyn Fraser (sister of Edmund). And that brings one to wonder whether perhaps it may have been Edmund's father, Patrick, who had actually bought the property in the first place! I do not know and I do not suppose anybody else does either.

Tammie Anderson continued his late brother's contracting business. He also had a keen interest in agriculture and the rearing of sheep. He took out a lease on the island of Papa Little, so around 1912 he sold part of his shop assets to a Yell man named James Smith, to devote more time to his agricultural interests. Tammie Anderson died suddenly in 1920, aged 55.

Jeemie Smith apparently had at least one shop in Yell before taking over the shop at Aith, but after only a few years he went back to Yell, before he eventually moved to Lerwick. Anyway, it was in Aith he met the girl who was to become his wife. Her name was Lillie Leslie, from Sandsound. She came to run the very first post office, set up around 1912. Jeemie Smith sold the Aith shop to another Yell merchant – James Clark, who I think had a shop in Ulsta. Anyway, around 1916, his nephew, Andrew D. Clark, was brought into the business. As far back as I remember Aith shop was run as Clark & Co. Andrew Clark was a shrewd business man and many went to him for advice on various problems. He was a county councillor and a Justice of the Peace. Fate had it ordained that he, too, was to meet his wife when he came to Aith. In September 1921, he married Christina Robertson, from the Grind in Clousta. He died in April 1966, aged 77 years.

Right up until the outbreak of the Second World War most goods still came by sea. One of the North of Scotland steamers called once a fortnight at Scalloway, Walls, Aith, Brae and Hillswick. In Aith Voe, the steamer anchored some distance off, between Pirliegert and Gudataing; two sixerns (similar to yoals which are now raced in the voes around Shetland in the summer months) did service as flit boats. Men were employed to transfer goods ashore and carry it into the stores.

Buying a pig

In those days quite a number of families fattened up a pig for slaughter in December. That home-cured ham had a special taste of its own when fried up with eggs in the voar of another year, when everybody had hard work to do with wheelbarrow and spade.

A farmer in Scalloway reared young piglets. Orders were sent in and those small, newly-weaned animals were shipped on the steamer in a big wooden crate, in which an armful of teased up buss (straw) had been added to help keep them warm, and perhaps help to make them feel more at home! Anybody expecting a piglet had to make sure to be on the pier at Gudataing to receive it.

Young pigs are not the easiest to handle. There is nothing to grip on to except a leg, an ear, or a curly tail. Just to touch a young pig causes it to squeal like mad. I remember my brother Robbie telling of one time he and our eldest brother, Tom – boys aged about 10 and 12 – had been sent with a rowing boat from Slyde up to Gudataing to collect two pigs (one of which was for a neighbour). They were armed with strong jute bags, each with the essential straw, into which they had to transfer the pigs from the wooden crate.

On this particular occasion Geordie Williamson from Clousta had come to collect his bit of bacon. He had a straw kishie, the mouth of which was partly sewn up with strong string, leaving just enough space through which to push the piglet. Poor peerie pig! All hell broke loose! There was no soft bed of straw for him to snuggle into to make him feel cosy. In a desperate bid for freedom he squealed like his last hour had come! And so, with the fore legs going like pistons, his extremely sharp clivs soon began to wear down the worn straw of which the kishie was made. You can imagine the scene. Soon, two small feet appeared, followed by a snout, and another scramble made enough room for the whole pig to bound out upon the ground. Geordie threw off the kishie with a string of oaths which the boys had never heard before, and made off after the poor peerie pig. All the others, of course, joined the chase and eventually caught up with it near the edge of the shun – where the marina is now.

Tammie Anderson felt sorry for Geordie as well as the pig, so took them both into his house where tea was made, and milk was warmed with oatmeal added and a dash of whisky for the porker! A bag with some straw was procured and the pig popped in, then the whole lot was popped into Geordie's kishie which, by then, was somewhat worse for wear. The boys, of course, had a laugh over the whole proceedings. They surely managed to bring home the bacon too, but not without a struggle. I feel sure that Geordie's peerie grice would have slept soundly in the straw all the way across the hill to Clousta (albeit with a sore head in the morning?)!

Relatives of Andrew D. Clark continued to run the shop at Aith up to the mid-1980s. The community-owned Eid Community Co-operative took over in 2002. By this time the building was in poor condition and in 2006 the business moved up the road to the newly renovated former knitwear factory. The original shop building was demolished in 2007.

29

The Unseen Stores

ONE day, while shopping in a supermarket at Lerwick, memories of long ago came flooding back to me of a totally different kind of shop – a small grocery shop at Gonfirth, South Delting, which was in existence from around 1925 to 1940.

The shop at Winnaness, Gonfirth, must have been unique; no goods were ever on display because the stores were kept upstairs in the room abune ben. It was run by Jonathan and Baabie Tulloch. In my opinion, Baabie was the driver of that project. By the time the shop was set up, Baabie was past middle age. She was always dressed in the fashion of her youth – long Shetland tweed skirt right down to her ankles and a long woollen jumper. We seldom saw her head bare for she always wore an all-over patterned cap. By the time I met them, the Winnaness folk would have been into their sixties perhaps, but when young I didn't bother to calculate a person's age. Elderly folk all looked the same age to me; and if advancing years added extra weight to their bodies, or if they lost weight and began to develop a few more wrinkles on their forehead I, for one, never seemed to notice. They seemed ageless!

Jonathan's job, I imagine, would have been standing by up at the road with his wheelbarrow, ready to meet the Voe van on its way with fresh bread from Adie's bakery (which was delivered twice a week to all the shops on the Westside). I do not know how Winnaness got their groceries. I seem to think it came from Tods of Lerwick. Some arrangement must have been made for its transport to Gonfirth. Anyway, it all had to be wheeled down to the house and carried upstairs to where it was stored.

At this time Gonfirth, Grobsness, and what was referred to as Da Wast Side (Houbanster, Ladie, etc.), were well populated. Winnaness was a handy place to buy cigarettes, matches and sweeties, besides all the rest. Jonathan was great at telling stories of his youthful exploits and everyone seemed eager to listen. It was all entertainment!

Baabie must have kept a ledger of sorts for she received quite a lot of private orders for hosiery from somebody sooth. Auntie Ellen continually did knitting for Baabie o' Winnaness – lots of matinee jackets, and woollen suits for small boys, besides every other sort of garment fashionable in those days. Once, I remember her doing an extra large jumper or vest, much too big to be stretched on an ordinary stretching board, so a piltik waand was pushed through both sleeves and hung on a hook on the gable of our house, where it was pulled into shape and left to dry!

Anyway, whenever Auntie Ellen had her hosiery ready, usually two of us children were sent to deliver it and to bring back the messages. We had a big wicker basket with a lid and a ropey baand which was adjusted to fit across our shoulders, as that sort of basket was specially made to be carried on one's back.

From Slyde it took an hour or more to reach Winnaness. We set off more or less on a straight cut over a very awkward steep and broken hill – full of brugs and broos and not such a thing as a sheep's gaet; the Fuglishuns was indeed a nasty piece of hill. When we reached the west edge of Quienster Loch the walking became somewhat easier, and soon we reached the ridge and could see Gonfirth lying below. Sometimes, we had a short rest there before proceeding downhill to join the Voe to Aith road, past the Brig o' Voxter and Gonfirth School, then down to Winnaness, where the house stood quite near the sea.

The greeting we got on arrival made up for the long hill trek. "Come in, peerie sweet loves. We'll gyit da kettle boilin an' hae some tae." So Grace (Baabie's sister who also lived there) got the blackened teapot set in among the embers of the open fire. That tea tasted strong and often had a reeky taste as well, but there was always a bowl of sugar on the table to give it a sweeter taste. Sometimes, when half-asleep – well within the twilight zone – I can still see it all, as it used to be, can still taste the strong tea and those straps of liquorice we always got.

Baabie then took our shopping basket containing the hosiery and an errand line (always written out before leaving home) and away upstairs she went to her private domain. Baabie seemed a happy person as usually she sang as she mounted the stairs.

Sometimes Grace and Jonathan would go outside to attend animals, leaving us in the but-end by ourselves. I was always one who enjoyed playing harmless practical jokes. I remember dropping a clod or a tattie into the jumble-kirn, which had a lid, and once I even threw in a handful of cold ashes. Dear me! Such are the things which make up memories of childhood! I soon came to see I had been foolish, knowing that if I was found out I would not feel good. So, no more tricks were played on such kind folk.

By and by, Baabie would come downstairs with the laden basket. The barter system still held sway so no money was ever handled (in my experience anyway). Occasionally, after I'd left school, Auntie Ellen would tell me to ask Baabie how we stood, meaning, were we solvent? Baabie's reply was always the same: "Plenty yit! Dere's plenty yit!" I have no recollection of any day of reckoning. Nevertheless, that could easily have been done without my knowledge.

After an hour's rest, and fortified with strong tea and thick slices of white loaf and crown biscuits, the time came to head for home. The basket had quite a bit of weight by this time but we were full of the vigour of youth so off we set, and as we left we heard more endearments. "Tak care, peerie jewels, hae peerie rests here an' dere," and always, the last we heard was, "Tak wir blissins tae your fok." Such kindliness was in that last message.

On the journey home we always took what we called da rodd gaet, trudging all the way up that long incline on the Voe to Aith road, until we at last reached Da Muckle Knowe. From there the road led downhill to East Burrafirth but we left the road at a place named Da Roadmen's Hoose and took a slant to the westward, past Longawater and the Lochs o' Burrafirth, keeping on flat ground until we reached the Sooth Grind and so down to our house. We had been away for three hours but time was no object then. There was always plenty of time to spare for anything we wanted to do.

Nevertheless, time did march on. Many changes were brought about with the outbreak of the Second World War. By then Baabie Tulloch would have been getting on in years. Rationing of certain foodstuffs would have made a lot of official paper work, and her hosiery market may have folded as well. So, I would imagine The Unseen Stores at Winnaness ceased to exist about 1940.

The Winnaness House

The house at Winnaness had rooms upstairs and a wooden roof covered with felt, which got a coating of tar every summer. Inside the but-end were two windows: one, of fair size and quite low, faced towards the east, up towards the road; the other window was smaller and set higher into the south gable so the room was always full of light.

On the left of the but door stood a washstand with a basin of water and a bar of soap in a dish. On a shelf underneath stood an auld benkled basin which often held some washed potatoes. I remember that basin of tatties, because Queen, their red-coloured dog, had a habit of sneaking across to help herself to a raw tattie and taking it back to her bed, in the only shadowy corner at the upper side of the open hearth. There she'd lie and shilk away at her tattie. We thought this was a queer thing for a dog to be eating. Our dogs at Slyde never had a chance to eat raw tatties but maybe Queen had got a taste of the unusual while still a puppy.

A fairly big, plain, wooden dresser stood opposite the washstand – opposite the fire. The top was always covered with tins and big jugs. Goodness knows what all was stored inside that piece of furniture – more than likely it could have been half a boll of flour meal and one of oatmeal.

Near the back window stood a jumble-kirn complete with kirn staff and lid – which served as Baabie's writing desk! The inside walls had been plastered and whitewashed. Calendars from many years back adorned the wall opposite the window. A restin chair stood along the wall, and a table, above which hung the rack full of fancy plates, while a row of cups hung underneath the rack.

Plain, low, wooden chairs stood on each side of the ben hearth. The chimney hadn't been built into the gable of the house but had what was referred to as a forced chimney. It seemed to be a wooden affair with a canopy towards the ceiling. I don't remember encountering reek or the sooty smell one sometimes met in some of those houses of long ago. This forced chimney was a stable structure firmly fixed to the gable with the cross-bar within, on which the crook was fixed for hanging pots and kettles.

I remember going along one day to find Baabie almost finished a stint at paper-hanging. She had got hold of a few outdated wallpaper pattern books from the Voe shop. She tore out the patterns one by one, mixed up some flour meal with cold water then added boiling water to make a good stiff paste which she then used to stick all those bits of wallpaper on to the sides and breast of the wooden chimney! The effect was original indeed, and Baabie was proud of her brainwave! It looked nice!

Grace Abernethy

Baabie's sister, Grace Abernethy, also lived at Winnaness, but she was of a quiet nature and didn't seem to say much – dominated perhaps by her sister. Grace was unmarried and seemed to be chief cook and tea cup washer! Grace was often baking bannocks.

Grace had a novel way of washing cups. She never had any washing-up bowl. She just took cups from the table, poured a little hot water into each and swilled it around the cup before emptying the water into the saucer. Next step was to give the cup a rock and roll movement in the saucer, and maybe she dried it. Then the washing-up water was either thrown on to the back of the open fire or into a washhand basin which stood on a washstand near the door. I'm sure some of those cups never got immersed in water from the day they were first used until perhaps they broke. They were all of the same pattern – a gold-coloured clover leaf on the side.

Another time I remember Grace frying lovely fresh herrings on the braand-iron over red hot embers. Each of us got a strong peat laid across our knees on which was laid a crusty fried herring. I think Jonathan ate his from a plate at the table but the women sat around with theirs on a peat! I don't remember whether we washed our fingers afterwards or not. More than likely we'd just have given them a 'dicht i da hochs o' wir wirset stockings'! Nobody worried about hygiene in those days. It's doubtful if that word had even been invented – even if it had, it certainly hadn't reached 'da back o' beyond o' Aest Burrafirt'! Anyway, that herring had a super taste. It must have done, or surely I widna be sitting here writing about it over eighty years on!

But what I remember most of all are those kind words spoken at Winnaness: "Come awa in, peerie sweet loves, we're blyde ta see you." In today's world, when on the telephone or maybe meeting up with an old friend, they'll ask how so and so is keeping: "Tell dem I wis axin for her (or him)." Somehow it doesn't have so deep a meaning as what Baabie o' Winnaness always called to us as we were leaving: "Tak wir blissins tae your fok!"

30
Other Shops

Floating shop

One other far away memory is of a man from Muckle Roe coming with a brown-sailed boat selling groceries. I seem to think his name was Jerry Hall, but in that I may be wrong. Tides were carefully noted, for I have been told he took his boat quite some way up the creek of the voe at East Burrafirth, which during spring tides ebbs out quite some way past Da Broch. (Only Meena's Burn keeps on rolling along, at a slower pace.) I was too young to take any part in meeting that floating shop from Muckle Roe. I would just have stood and looked.

Selkieburn Shop

I have only one memory of being at the shop in Selkieburn – a small shed built on the west gable of the house. That shop had apparently been set up by Nannie Tait (not the same Nannie from Hametoon who became my teacher) sometime towards the end of the 19th century. Her husband, Johnnie Tait, was a fisherman. Very often he was absent from home, so it was usually Nannie, who could handle a boat as well as any man, who would set off for Brae for a load of foodstuffs for her shop. I daresay a moderate morning would have been chosen for the trip. She took two young boys, maybe aged twelve to fourteen, as her crew. At first it would perhaps have been one of her youngest sons and another fellow. Nannie o' Selkieburn gave many a boy their first lessons on how to handle a boat wearing a dipping-lug sail. A trip to Brae would have been enjoyed very much by those young budding seamen.

Of course, it wasn't all plain sailing. The wind could rise quite quickly, making the journey back to East Burrafirth a nasty business. Many a story has been lost; but one time when Johnnie Tait, Nannie's husband, was in charge of the boat he had to spend a night on the Isle of Linga dodging out a snowstorm. There has never, to my knowledge, been any kind of lodgings on Linga, apart from maybe a crö for some ewes, so it widda been an interesting night for Johnnie!

Haa o' Braewick shop

Another shop in Aith had been run by a Thomas Abernethy in a small building down at the seashore, on the croft known as the Haa o' Braewick. But that was before I can remember. Tammie Abernethy died in 1916; quite a number of his family had predeceased him. I can only remember his eldest daughter Jessie, who lived alone for years at the Haa. She died around 1946.

Section 5

Early Education

31

Education in the East Burrafirth Area

SEVERAL schools were open in the Aithsting area before any school was built in Aith. I have gathered a little history about some of them.

John Johnson (John o' da Holm) 1809-1889

Sometime before proper schools had been built in this district, a man named John Johnson, who had been born at Huxter in Weisdale in 1809, came along. He had been a seaman until that became impossible after he lost his right hand. In the census returns he is stated to be a disabled navy pensioner, with a pension of 3d per day. But then, in those days, folk managed to live on very little money. Somewhere along the line he had been fitted with an iron hook affair, attached to his right forearm.

I know nothing of his early life, but in the 1851 census I found him living with his wife Margaret Tait, and two children, Erasmus (5) and Helen (2), at Braewick, Aith – Margaret's birthplace. His age was given as 42 and his wife was 29. I do not know how he met his wife but they were married in Weisdale, in 1844. Sometime before 1861 this family moved across Aith Voe to a croft named The Holm – so named because a holm lies immediately offshore – at the mouth of East Burrafirth Voe. Two of his daughters married Balfour brothers from Houbanster.

At first, I believe he began going to various houses where children were keen to learn, and whose parents let their children attend. Whether those lessons would have been on a regular basis or not, I cannot say. I think some parents helped things along by paying the teacher in kind, and in John o' da

Holm's case he, being disabled, got a lot of help getting peats cut and cured and, more than likely, other assistance too.

John was very partial to telling tall tales. One was that he had once shot 99 starlings on a bear's back. When asked, "Whit wye wis it no a hunder?" he was reputed to answer, "Wid I sin my soul for the sake o' ee stirling?" When he died, very suddenly, one of his sons-in-law said, "No more lies will come oot o' his mooth." So I better get on with some details about John o' da Holm's schools!

School at Hestataing

Soon after the Education Act was passed, a small stone-built school got erected at Hestataing. This is said to have been the first school in this district. At that time there apparently were two small crofts at Hestataing. One house had been near the shore, where the wast noost is, while the other small dwelling, known as Da Gyill, lay inside the hill daek. The occupants of both houses were father and son, Tirval and Peter Goudie, whose ancestors had been born in South Nesting. The Gyill house was demolished by army practice during the Second World War.

Anyway, the so-called school was built where the barn at Hestataing now stands, so we have been told. To be honest, it's not much of a building today – what it was like over 100 years earlier, I wouldn't really care to think. However, what you never know you never miss and I'm sure the opportunity to learn would have been quite a step in the rural community. Whether all the bairns had the same opinion is debatable – that would be one thing that's likely never to change!

Hestataing would have been a handy enough site for a school as it lay halfway between Aith and East Burrafirth. Boys from the west side of Aith Voe rowed across in a small boat, so eager were they to learn and, I daresay, John Johnson would have been keen to teach. Perhaps those scholars came on a rota basis but I have no way of knowing.

We can only guess what form the lessons took. There certainly would have been no jotters, but slates and slate pencils may have been the order of the day. It is generally thought that children of those days would have been taught shorter catechism. What's that? I hear you say. It was a book of questions and answers forming a brief summary of the basics of the principles of Christianity; and for all I know there may have been other books of the same sort but on different subjects.

They also learned spelling, poetry and all those horrible never-ending tables. Goodness knows what else. As John Johnson had been a seaman, and knowing that almost all his pupils would go to sea, maybe he gave them some idea on how to box the compass too.

I feel sorry now, that I never thought of asking my father more about his schooling days. He had been a pupil of John o' da Holm and often spoke of his old teacher.

School at Winnaness

Maybe about the same time as a school was built at Hestataing, another school got built on the Ayre o' Voxter, just below South Voxter (in South Delting). If you stop your car on the corner below where the Gonfirth School and schoolhouse stand, you will see what remains of that old school. John o' da Holm taught there too. Like the one at Hestataing it would have had a thatched roof and maybe a pane of glass for a skylight. Apparently the door always stood open, especially in summer time –to let in fresh air I presume, for it could have been pretty crowded sometimes.

I have discovered that when the peerie skule had been built on the Ayre o' Voxter, it had been erected so near the sea that extra high tides flowed into the building. I imagine the earthen floor would always have been dampish; children and teachers of that age were well used to damp floors and may well have had flat slabs of stone laid down in the wettest places. It was all part of the play!

32

East Burrafirth School

ABOUT 1906, a croft house known as Da Gutters, in East Burrafirth, became vacant so the Education Authority rented it for use as a school until 1945, when it closed and the pupils were driven to Aith.

In recent years quite a number of old school photographs have appeared, with many displayed at various History Group projects, thereby arousing much interest. But the peerie side-skule at East Burrafirth was sadly neglected by the photographer, who apparently came north regularly from Blackpool to take pictures of school groups. The reason we got left out may well have been lack of a road, or perhaps he would not have known such a school existed in such an out-of-the-way place. It is very disappointing not to have even one photograph to study and comment on. As far as I know, no one ever came to take photos at East Burrafirth – even when a road did eventually open up the place. The only picture I have of children at our school was taken by Babsy Tait from Hametoon around 1932 – by which time my school days were over.

Side-schools are apt to get overlooked, and perhaps are not worth a mention as far as history goes. I have been asked more than once "And what school did you attend?" A look of surprise would cross their faces when I tried to tell them of a side-school at East Burrafirth. Most folk hadn't known such an out-of-the-way place existed. Little wonder, I daresay, for before motor cars came along there was no reason for people to follow all by-ways and visit out-of-the-way townships.

Those of you who may have in your possession copies of Manson's *Shetland Almanac* from those years before the Second World War, will discover a list of all schools in Shetland. Fifteen of them are listed as side-

1932: East Burrafirth school with outside toilet. On the left is the "black end" – notice the window is blocked up with stones. The black end is where the school peats were stored, as well as the Hametoon tatties. The classroom was on the right of the door; it had a window at the front and two skylights on the back. Lollie Tait (Hametoon) is standing in the playground!

schools. There is also a list of teachers' names and how many pupils attended each school. All over the Shetland Islands there were isolated townships where there were no roads, but in spite of that disadvantage some places, especially where the ground was fertile, were well populated so there were always quite a number of school-age children.

I think the very first teacher at East Burrafirth would have been Robbie Hunter from Quienster, followed for a year or so by Robbie's brother John, neither of whom had teacher training except perhaps what they had picked up from their teachers at Gonfirth. John Hunter was posted to teach at Eshaness around 1912 after which Robbie Leask from Scord, Aith, and some other young lad from Aith took turns at trying to drum some learning into those at East Burrafirth. This apparently proved unsatisfactory. Little beyond school leaving age themselves, they found it an uneasy task trying to keep rule on those hooligans who ganged up against them. It ended up that my parents took my brothers Jeemie and Johnnie and my sister Liza away from East Burrafirth school and sent them across the hill to Gonfirth. I'm not certain, but I think our cousin Peter, about a year younger than Liza, was bundled off to Gonfirth too – when he was maybe eight years old. The stories Liza used to tell of how they ganged up against their youthful teachers, and the pranks they played were really past a joke for they were mischief-bent instead of applying themselves to their lessons. No wonder my parents took drastic action!

Teachers at East Burrafirth

APART from Nannie Tait, I remember two other teachers at East Burrafirth.

Jeannie Bain

In 1934, because of an outbreak of scarlet fever amongst the inmates of the Hametoon, Nannie, naturally, was banned from teaching so someone had to be found to keep the small school in operation.

A young woman came from Lerwick to take over for a short time that summer. Her name was Jeannie Bain; she got accommodation at Hestataing beside the Sandison family. She was transported by rowing boat from the Hestataing east noost across to the Wasthoose noost. The boatman was usually young Jeemie Sandison, though sometimes it would have been his father. On one trip a lobster was discovered ebbed up among the tang at the Wasthoose side. It measured 34 inches (85.4cm) from claw to tail, so I expect the Sandison family would have enjoyed a taste of seafood! Hopefully Jeannie would have got a tasting too. Jeannie taught the children that year from after the holidays at Easter until the summer holidays.

Yet again, as so often happens, fate had it ordained that, through coming to teach at the small side-school, Jeannie met the man destined to become her husband. His name was Peter Anderson, from Voehead, Aith – a son of Faider's brother John Anderson, and Jemima Blance. Peter had fallen ill while working as a shepherd with his brother-in-law in Brechin, so had not long returned home to recuperate when he met Jeannie. Theirs was a long courtship and they married in February 1941. The car taking Peter and his best man to Lerwick got stuck in snow at Wormadale so by the time they had shoved and dug the car up the hill they were pretty late for the ceremony. They spent most of their married life at East Gate, and Jeannie lived at East Burrafirth until her death, in 1999.

Willa Laurenson

Later on, maybe about 1938, when Nannie Tait had a spell of poor health, another woman helped out with teaching. Her name was Willa Laurenson who, before her marriage to George Laurenson, had been infant teacher at Aith School. Her maiden name was Tait. She lived in Twatt and used a motorcycle as a method of transport. After her marriage she and her husband lived at Sunnybank, near Aith shop.

While helping out teaching at East Burrafirth she left her motorcycle in the quarry at Da Burgans. From the pier down at the shore she was transported across in a very small flat-bottomed skyiff – the distance across the narrow section of voe between Burgans and Hametoon piers is not great. The boatman in this case was Frankie Tait from the Hametoon, a lad aged about 13, who was one of the school pupils.

34

School for Aith

A LETTER had been drafted to the Education Authority by Thomas Anderson and Andrew Clark in the hope that the need for a school to be built in Aith would get priority attention. That letter had more or less been ignored.

A public meeting of ratepayers and parents was held on 2nd February, 1919, in the North Store of Gudataing. It had come to light that certain members of the council were against a school being erected down near the head of Aith Voe. A committee was formed, and a letter drafted and sent to the Education Authority with reference to the original petition and asking that they send a delegation to visit the district and ascertain the seriousness of the situation for themselves. The Authority decided to do nothing in the matter until the Master of Works had visited the district and made an estimate of the costs, etc.

The matter apparently came before a meeting in September 1921, but no decision was reached. Much ill-feeling arose between the people in Aith and the Education Authority. However, negotiations took place between the Education Authority and the Minister of Defence, concerning procuring the barracks on Swaarback Head to be put to good use as a school at Aith.

So maybe I need to go right back to when big guns got set up on Swaarback Head, on the north end of the Isle of Vementry, early in the 1914-18 war. They were there as a protection for a naval fleet which was stationed in Busta Voe. Of course, accommodation for the guns' crews was also erected. I understand this consisted of quite a fair-sized wooden hut to serve as barracks. After the end of hostilities that building was dismantled. All the wooden sections would have been transported down a steep slope to the inlet of Northravoe and from there transferred to sixerns, which would have taken them up to the head of Aith Voe.

I assume those wooden portions would have been off-loaded at high tide on to the Ayre o' Gudataing, right below where the school was to be erected. I do not know who had the contract for the re-erecting of those hut sections. No doubt it would have been done by local men. I do not know who would have been our district councillor at that time. I do know that Tammie Anderson from Vementry had been Aithsting's representative up to the time of his sudden death at Lerwick, aged 54 years, in 1920.

Enough space was provided for two fair-sized classrooms, besides living quarters for the teacher William Laurenson, his mother, his sister Lizzie and brother George. I have been told the school was ready by the end of 1921 and opened for its first intake of 27 pupils after the Christmas holidays, on 16th January, 1922. William Laurenson had a long career at Aith School – 37 years. One of my daughters recalls running home from her first day at school clutching a florin given to her by Mr Laurenson to mark the start of her education. On his retiral, in 1959, he and his sister moved to Lerwick; he passed away on 3rd December, 1981, aged 85.

When the first school got erected at Aith, there was, of course, no water on tap. Water had to be carried from a well, perhaps by the school cleaner, but I am not certain about that. I shouldn't be surprised to learn that perhaps a couple of the older boys would have done that job. I have been told that the first cleaner was Katie Anderson, from the Voehead. One of her tasks was to carry slop-buckets from the toilets every afternoon down to the shore and empty the contents into the sea. No doubt the sillocks would have disposed of the waste, but that is how it was when life was lived in the raw. Today's youth may find this hard to believe. Very few folk born in Shetland after 1950 know anything of how things were done before flush toilets came into use. In this district that would have been after mains water arrived in the autumn of 1955.

We, who are old enough to remember, feel so glad to have lived through the age from very primitive conditions and to have seen the progress of modern technology. Many things in common use by the youth of the present time are quite beyond my understanding – computers, etc. (I was especially amazed at the first e-mail correspondence I had with an old pen pal from New Zealand. In days gone by, it would be weeks before I would receive a reply to my letter. However, I was astonished when a reply came within a day, when I had my daughter send a message by e-mail!) Mankind is never satisfied. Scientists are forever bent on proving themselves that one step ahead. Nowadays there could be too many buttons to press. I trust the time will never come when someone will press the wrong button; if only to prove that he or she is right.

In 1935, a new concrete school and schoolhouse were built. The former closed as a school in 1982; for several years it was the home of Aith Social Club and is currently the Auld Skule Recycling Centre. The schoolhouse is now private property.

In Shetland today, children who have an aptitude for further education certainly have the opportunity to follow on into any of the professions in which they have an interest. It was not always so. In my generation only a very few ambitious children were lucky enough to have the necessary financial backing. Talking to youngsters today, however, it becomes apparent at times that they have too many choices, as many appear to follow a career path early on, only to discover that this is not as they wish. We did not have this choice. But as ever, people are often hard to please, the grass is greener saying comes to mind, that is one thing that remains the same. If you do find a job you enjoy and is rewarding, not essentially financially but personally, you are lucky indeed. Shetland should be proud of the education opportunities that it provides for children. The sad story is that many of these highly educated adults are leaving Shetland as they struggle to find challenging employment within the isles. This will undoubtedly lead to an ageing generation, and will the schools require to expand as much as in the past? A question that only time will answer.

35

The Closing of East Burrafirth School

I DISCOVERED, only in 1996, something which was news to me – that sometime shortly after the road got laid down through East Burrafirth there had been plans to build a new school. Apparently a couple of men connected with the Zetland Education Authority came out to survey for a suitable site. They had their eyes on a flat piece of land just below the road on the west side of the Mill Brig. They met with opposition as that bit of ground, a good fertile rig belonging to the Hametoon croft, was still under cultivation. It went under the name of Da Bread Pieces. I'm not sure whether at one time, long ago, it may have grown good corn from which oatmeal would have been ground at the mill. No way were the Hametoon folk giving up a good rig for the building of another school. What was wrong, anyway, with the old school etc? I was also told that there was no objection from the tenant of The Haa croft, for a site somewhere out on ground beyond where the Aest Gaet house stood.

But anyway, nothing came of all those plans, for only a year later the Second World War broke out, which changed so many things and lots of the old way of life disappeared for ever. By then, of course, the writing was on the wall. Zetland Education Authority had made their decision to close the East Burrafirth School and transport the pupils to Aith. Most of the parents went stark mad at such a plan, and got up in arms. Quite unable to see that to have their children driven to a better school would be an asset in many ways, they dug their heels in!

At that time, Mr Andrew Clark from Gudataing was our county councillor. Somehow the folk in Burrafirth felt he had let them down and laid the blame on him for allowing the peerie skule to be closed; so much so, that when election time came around and Mr John Sutherland from Bixter stood against Mr Clark, everyone from East Burrafirth set out for Bixter to cast their votes and thereby managed to oust Clark. Mind you, that was all done out of spite, for Clark was the favoured candidate. Later perhaps, some of them became aware that they had maybe gone and cut off their noses to spite their faces. Quite a few folk had been in the habit of going to Mr Clark for advice and help in writing official letters. So all the oncarry only caused bad feeling between the two districts.

The closing of the school was something inevitable anyway, but all those years ago people resented change and were unable to accept it with good grace. I wonder what some of those people of a bygone age would think if they could walk around any of today's modern schools.

Jeannie Anderson (nee Bain) was the teacher when the school closed for good in November 1945. I wonder why the pupils weren't enrolled at Aith at the end of August when the new term began. I have been unable to discover the reason why. Of course, the intake of 13 pupils, of various ages, into the classes of Aith might perhaps have required some adjustment so that each child could be settled into his or her rightful place.

The last pupils at East Burrafirth side school were: Doris Eunson (12), South Lea; Kenny (11) and Douglas (9) Henry, Holm; Laurence (12), Tammie (10) and Bobbie (6) Tait, Hametoon; Elsie (10) and Morris (6) Tait, Wasthoose; Wilma (9), Margaret (7) and Joyce (5) Anderson, Upper Pund; Rhoda Tulloch (10), Hoit and Patsy Tait (6), Roadside.

I had a chat with Jeannie Anderson a few weeks before I wrote this, in 1996, and she told me that it was Geordie Smith, from North Gardie in Aith, with his lorry, who had been employed to transport all the school equipment from East Burrafirth to Aith School. There was no gate or road wide enough to allow the lorry to get down anywhere near the school, so all the gear had to be humped up to the road. Not a soul came out to offer any assistance; everybody kept out of sight – out of spite! Jeannie had to fetch her husband to help carry desks and cupboards. Everybody was so mad to have lost the battle. They surely couldn't (or wouldn't) swallow their pride and welcome a new era.

I think the resentment may have rubbed off on to some of the children too. During the summer holidays of 1945, Elsie Tait had come for a week or two to stay with me at South Houll, Weisdale, where I was living at that time. I can still remember her sitting on a stool warming her toes on the stove fender, the evening before she was to go back home, and saying, "I'm no lookin forward ta goin ta dat Aith Skule; I ken we'll be tormented an looked doon on!" I tried to reassure her that she shouldn't feel that way – just to remember she was as good, if not better, than any other child. "Juist du stick up for desell, an it'll be aa right. Don't du forgyit dat."

Things have changed now, but I can well remember that feeling of inferiority which we felt towards those folk who lived up around the head of Aith Voe. We clodhoppers from East Burrafirth seemed to have nothing, while Aith had everything – a shop and post office, a church, a hall and a better school. It was, of course, all in our minds, for a kind, friendly lot of folk lived up around the Gudataing area and we were never ever made to feel strangers. We always called along some of our relations living near the shop for a cup of tea before setting out for home with a basket of messages on our back.

Yet, with hindsight, I realise that we who lived at East Burrafirth did have advantages over those folk in Aith; it was from Burrafirth that they purchased good fat hogs for salting down for reestit mutton, and pullets' eggs for baking their Christmas cakes. That was the real situation, though in those years of long ago we somehow felt we were laughed at behind our backs. How could we have been so touchy and foolish! We much preferred going to Houbanster and the Gonfirth area where everybody was so very down to earth, such kindly people who never put on any airs or graces, where we always felt so very much at home.

Gonfirth School was closed in 1946. The two girls living at Grobsness had reached the age of leaving (fourteen) – their names were Lilly Balfour and Winnie Anderson. Mrs Edith Comloquoy (a native of Orkney) reached retiring age earlier on that year. She had been teacher at Gonfirth since 1919, so quite a number of children had been taught by her in that time. She and her daughter Olga moved to Whiteness shortly after the school closed.

So now I feel I have come to the end of schooling. As I now pass on to more old history I have to hoist my sail on a different tack; often as my thoughts wander I wonder where I will make land and sometimes it even surprises myself as I make landfall somewhere within my box of memories that I had entirely forgotten existed. It's like finding my own New World!

Section 6

Clousta

36

The People Who Lived at Bonhouse

I HAVE many memories of holidays spent at Bonhouse, Clousta. Those childhood memories are very pleasant to recall; sometimes, in my dreams I get transported to that special place and meet again some of those kindly caring folk – all now gone to their rest. My first visit was for Uncle Christie's wedding to Mimie Ellen Tait, but first a bit of background about Bonhouse, and the people living there when I first visited.

Betty Tait (nee Doull) – Mam o' Bonhouse (1855-1947)

Mimie Ellen's mother (always known as Betty Doull although she had been Mrs Tait for many a year) lived at Bonhouse. She would have been in her mid-seventies by the time I was first there, still a robust, hardworking woman. She had had a hard young life and had to toil always with her nose at the grindstone. Many years later, after Betty had gone to her rest, I was told that as a younger woman Betty had been a proper tartar when the need arose. I was never aware of it, for to me she was kindness itself, and somehow took the place of a grandmother; we always referred to her as Mam o' Bonhouse. She passed on to me her outlook on life.

Betty had been born in November 1855, at a croft known as Da Millgaets in Brindister, Aithsting. Her parents were Anthony Doull and Elizabeth Anderson. As far as I know Betty had no brothers, but I can remember her speaking of her two sisters. One, whose name was Nannie, married a man named Tammie Nicolson from Twatt. That couple eventually settled in Scalloway.

The other sister, named Baabie, emigrated to Australia sometime around the 1870s. Apparently Betty had a strong desire to join this sister, but she told me how it came about that she felt her destiny didn't lie down under in that land of opportunity. The schoolmaster at Sandness acted as emigration agent, so those who wished to put their names forward went to him to have the necessary papers filled up. Betty, along with others, set off on foot to Sandness (though there could have been a chance to cross from West Burrafirth to Sandness by boat). Somehow those documents got lost along the way to whichever place they had been sent. So Betty got a message to come again to Sandness. She set out with the eagerness of youth, but it laid on a day of heavy snowfall, a proper 'moorie caavie', and that was seen as an omen not to attempt to emigrate. Being a believer that our destiny is indeed laid in our laps, I think Betty was right, so her future lay at Bonhouse in Clousta, and not in sunny Australia.

I do not know exactly when Betty first came to Bonhouse, but she came first of all as a servant to John Tait and his wife Helen, when they were both well advanced in years. Their shop at Bonhouse was then run by their eldest son Andrew, a widower. He also had a young lad as a servant. Betty told of one day they had been sent to da Ness o' Clousta to transport some faels (divots) in straw kishies to build up a surround for a midden. Like all, or most, young fellows, he took a notion to swing his weight on the back of Betty's kishie. "Heth, he didna try dat a second time." I bet he didna, for I imagine Betty could use her fists on anyone who annoyed her. She had had a tough upbringing, which more than likely stood her in good stead more than once, and she is said to have been well able to use her tongue too.

Another story she would tell was of one winter's evening when she had gone to fetch water from the well, which was a bit away from the house. Starlight was her only guide in a moonless sky. She had bent down to fill her second wooden daffik when she became aware of the form of someone, or something, between her line of vision and the starlit sky. As she was bending down this image bent down too; as she straightened up it straightened too. She was at a loss to know who or what it might be. So, gathering her wits, she decided to throw the water which was in her daffik over whatever it happened to be! She had wondered at first if it might be "Da mukkle deevil himsell"! But she stood her ground, in silence. It's anyone's guess who would have got the biggest shock, for the image at the well turned out to be a young local man who'd returned home that very day from the whaling at Greenland! He was on his way to visit Betty's folk and maybe he was a klik. She didn't disclose his name and now I feel sorry I didn't ask more.

Andrew had been a widower for a number of years before Betty Doull came on the scene. His eldest daughter Catherine (always referred to as Wir Kaatrin) was only a year younger than Betty. I have no idea when Andrew and Betty became attracted to each other but she told me of this dream she had one night in which Andrew Tait presented her with a knife! Next morning, she retold her dream to his daughters. "Oh, Betty, du's gaen tae gyit a widow man; wha wis it gae dee a knife? Come on, tell wis!" "Bit I watched dat I never telt dem," said the shrewd Betty, though I have no doubt at all that they smelt a rat, and guessed alright which way the wind blew. I can only guess, for Betty didn't tell me any more. The marriage didn't take place till a few years later.

In December 1883, Andrew's daughter Kaatrin and his son John both got married. Not long afterwards, Kaatrin and her husband, John Jamieson, set off for Queensland, while John decided to take his wife (another Betty) to live in the family home at Bonhouse.

Perhaps Andrew maybe then decided that Betty Doull was a person well worth holding on to? And who can tell, Betty might well have seen the advantages of becoming Andrew's second wife, regardless of the huge gap between their ages. He was 57 and Betty was 31 when they got wed at Lerwick, in July 1887. I remember being told that nobody knew for certain that they intended getting married, so when they returned to Bonhouse (via a boat from Scalloway to Bixter then on foot to Clousta) and announced they were man and wife, it fairly set the cat among the chickens! Feathers began to fly in all directions! No way could two women rule the roost! By this time, John Tait and his wife had two young children, but it appears they had no option but to move out. They ended up at the Greenmeadow, but I don't know if it was vacant at the time or if they baled out somewhere else first.

We only heard Betty Doull's side of the story. Everything was divided – kye, sheep, ducks and hens, and all the household goods were separated too, though each side kept their own dog! Betty Doull told of how auld Helen's wedding plaid also got torn in half. I didn't believe that; though one can never tell. Maybe both Bettys yanked it apart in a frenzy of temper! There's no telling what can take place when two tirn wives let go of themselves!

Andrew Tait died in 1907, aged 77, so Betty was a widow, aged 52. None of the three children – Matthew, Mimie Ellen and Freddy – was old enough to keep the shop business afloat. Betty suffered the disadvantage of having had no opportunity of getting any schooling so she was unable even to sign her own name and I don't think she could make much of reading even the printed word. Mimie Ellen would sometimes read stories, or articles from *The Shetland Times* or whatever. Sometimes Betty would sit with a big print Bible, a lot of which she could repeat from memory. She could count alright, and all in all she was a very intelligent woman and certainly nobody's fool, scared of nothing.

The last time I saw Mam o' Bonhouse was only a few months before she died. By then she was nearing her 91st birthday, her memory as clear as a bell. I said, "You must feel you've been a long, long time on this earth?"

"Na na! It doesna seem lang ava; du maun mind a lok o' dat time wis spent sleepin; an anidder thing I can tell dee, life is just laek da wadder – sometimes da sun'll shine an du'll not hae a care in da world; dan da cloods will start biggin up intae da ert an du'll winder what's comin. Sometimes da sky will darken an dy tochts will be darkened tü, winderin what's comin. Even dan it can clear awa whan da mön rises! Yet agen, dir edder times storm cloods will send a doontöm a rain an a gale du canna stand up in. But if du haes patience, aa dat'll blaa by tü, and du'll fin da sun will shine agen an aa will seem bright." I've never forgotten Betty's words and have proved them to be true, time and time again.

Betty passed away peacefully at Bonhouse, in March 1947. The local undertaker was Fraser Hughson; he was employed by Clark & Co. and lived nearby at Valleyfield, Aith. When Betty passed away, Uncle Christie took his staff in his hand and walked along a trukkit gaet across the hill from Clousta, although, at that time there was a deep snow over all of Shetland. On reaching Aith, a message was sent to Alec Leask at East Burrafirth to collect the coffin at the Gudataing pier and transport it on his motorboat to Clousta, through Cribba Sound. On the funeral day, Alec fetched the coffin from the noost at Bonhouse to the head of Aith Voe. A service was held in Aith Kirk and Betty was laid to rest in the cemetery on a fine sunshiny day which made the snow sparkle – as if with diamonds!

That year Shetland's roads were blocked by deep snow; almost all transport had to be by sea. The snow had a hard frozen crust which stayed that way for six weeks, with no wind and brilliant sunshine most days.

Not long afterwards, another Clousta woman passed away, so Alec's services were again required. This time the coffin was transported by horse and sledge from Aith to the cemetery at Twatt. She was the wife of Fraser Jamieson from Setter; her maiden name had been Jerimina (Meena) Henry, originally from Noonsbrough.

So much local history has now been lost. It is one of my regrets that I didn't start keeping a diary from my early teenage years but in those days not many people of my generation did so. I keep all my diaries; perhaps there might indeed be an interest in them sometime in the future.

May 1926: Christie Anderson, Mimie Ellen Anderson, Betty Tait. They were dressed for "kirkning" – first church attendance following marriage.

Mimie Ellen (1891-1964)

Jemima Helen Brown Tait was the only daughter of Andrew Tait and his second wife, Betty Doull. Mimie Ellen (we referred to her by that name to distinguish her from our two other Auntie Mimies – one at Sandsound and one at the Voehead, Aith) had been engaged to marry John Tait from Pirliegert, Aith, but John, like so many more, was lost at sea during the First World War.

Mimie Ellen had never seen her two half-sisters from her father's first marriage. Nevertheless, Mimie Ellen and Kaatrin wrote letters to each other regularly. Mimie Ellen would give me Kaatrin's letters to read. Towards the end of her life those letters were full of memories of her youth, and those friends from her girlhood whom she longed to meet again, and always wished she could visit her birthplace once more. In those days that wish could never be achieved, but at least she would have appreciated the letters Mimie Ellen sent. I daresay Mimie Ellen felt sorry too that she had no opportunity to see her sister so far away, though her brother Freddy met her once or twice.

Her other half-sister was also named Jemima Helen. She had married a Nicolson man from Nesting and emigrated to America. A tragedy overtook that family as Jemima Helen was killed when she was in a buggy drawn by a runaway pony, leaving a little girl under a year old. I think that accident occurred before Mimie Ellen had been born, so she was named after her half-sister. A photograph of that peerie lass in America stood on a dressing-table upstairs at Bonhouse for years, and the photograph of a memorial card for Jemima Tait hung on Mimie Ellen's bedroom wall.

Those big families of long ago soon scattered, yet there was always at least one who stayed at home to look after ageing parents. One wonders how often those who stayed might indeed have longed to spread their wings and fly away too. But that was how things were. Mimie Ellen certainly stayed on in the old home but was forever reaching out to her faraway relations and always tried to keep in touch with everybody. She was always writing letters and always had her book of postage stamps handy as well, all ready for the postman.

Mimie Ellen wasn't a house-proud woman. Dust and truss lying around didn't get on her nerves at all. Even so, there were certain things she never failed to keep shining and, if visitors were expected, the linoleum which covered the floor got a swipe over with a big swab. So long as what might be seen by a visitor was clean there was no worry about what dust and guttery footmarks might be elsewhere.

Every Saturday evening she washed the floor with a big swab, made from an old woollen jumper in which the grit from the floor got entangled, so that when it was wrung out and given a shake one could hear the sandy soil dancing under the restin chair! Somehow, Mimie Ellen never bothered to sweep the floor before the process of washing. Next, latish on, after the washing of the floor, she got out her tin of Brasso and shone up a pair of brass candlesticks which took pride of place on the but mantelpiece. All the tins and other knick-knacks which stood there often just got a flick with a duster. She knew it was indeed a losing battle.

I remember one time Mimie Ellen was frying saucermeat on the stove when a clod from Christie's kishie jumped into the pan. She just flicked it out and on to the feeder of the stove and right into the blazing fire.

Sometimes the frying pan would perhaps have been left standing to cool, across the corner of the peat box. Once, Christie arrived with his burden of peats and quickly set the pan on the cushion of another muckle wicker chair which stood opposite the restin chair – quite near the stove. On lifting the frying pan back on to the peat box he noticed a sooty mark on the cushion. He quickly turned the cushion upside down so nobody noticed.

Mimie Ellen had taken a minor stroke in 1945; was very upset and disorientated for a while, but she recovered and through time became very much like her old self, until early in 1961, when she took a heavy stroke, after which she had to be admitted to Brevik Hospital in Lerwick.

It was sad to see her made so helpless, but she was well attended by the nursing staff there, until she passed away in March 1964, aged 73.

Uncle Christie (1884-1952)

Uncle Christie was my father's second youngest brother. He was a tall man and so unlike my father you wouldn't have thought they were brothers at all. I have been told that as a young man he had intended getting wed to a Sarah Nicolson from Twatt (a relation of his own) but she died quite young so, like so many other plans, that was never realised.

Unlike his brothers who were all seamen, Christie's interest lay on the land, working with animals. He had worked at various places and for some years before his marriage had been employed, and lived, at the croft of Aithsness, by his cousin Jeemie Anderson. He attended Clousta Kirk where I daresay he met Mimie Ellen, but I never thought to ask into that bit of history.

Before his marriage took place, Uncle Christie came every fortnight across to our home at Slyde and we bairns adored him; he had such a kindly disposition towards children, and we were lucky, too, in his choice of a wife for Mimie Ellen was just a proper bairn's boddy. It was unfortunate they had no family of their own. Maybe they were disappointed, but I don't know; they both had the knack of reaching out to children – anybody's children. Mimie Ellen would chuckle and laugh over the forthright sayings of young bairns.

Christie was not a lover of hens, but had to tolerate them in spite of them scratching up his newly set cabbage plants and other things besides. I recall one summer's day Mimie Ellen had gone away somewhere. There was a hen with a laachter of young chickens roaming around on the byre floor. The byre at Bonhouse was quite a modern building for that day and age; it was in no way cramped or dark. It had a concrete floor and oiler in which, especially in summer, a fair amount of slurry would gather. Anyway, I think Christie had awakened from his nap and made for the byre to wheel out what was gathered in the oiler. Lo and behold, there were four of Betty's precious chickens stuck among the slurry with the mother hen in great distress. I suppose he did the thing which first came into his mind. I can see him yet, in my mind's eye, taking hold of a big square-mouthed shovel, lifting the four unlucky chicks (slurry and all) and tilting them out on a big flat stone on top of the yard daek – thinking no doubt that they would soon dry off in the sun and wind. Of course, the mother hen was more upset than ever, her poor peerie chickens were too high up for her to see them and they were chirping louder than ever too.

Betty soon appeared and I bet she wasn't at all pleased. She lifted them one by one from off their stony platform into the bight of her apron and made for the house. I looked in shortly afterwards and there was Betty washing the chickens' feet and under feathers in a big soup plate of warm soapy water, after which she got them into a box under the stove – all the while muttering to herself. Christie, on coming in for his tea, heard them pleepin and asked, "Ir dey still livin?" He seemed surprised. Betty hadn't been pleased at all and who could blame her, though I don't think she said a word openly. No doubt Mimie Ellen would have heard all about what a stupid lot those Andersons were!

By 1952 plans had been made to fix up the house at Bonhouse, so it had been arranged that they would move into the house at Skyurds while this was done. On the Sunday before the Bonhouse folk flit to Skyurds, Jeemie took me and our two eldest children, Jeemsie and Thelma, across to Bonhouse. I was dismayed at noticing how haggard Uncle Christie looked, not in his usual cheery manner at all, so very unlike himself, especially when he had bairns for company. I put the reason down to the fact that he had been up part of the night attending a heifer at her first calving. When, in the afternoon, the time came to milk his young cow he wasn't feeling like doing so. Freddy and his wife Maggie were there and Mimie Ellen accompanied them to the byre. So,

Circa 1930: in the Bonhouse back yard. Left to right: Betty, Matthew and Mimie Ellen – Matthew must have been home on holiday from Glasgow.

of course, our bairns wanted to go there too, to view the new calf. Nae winder Blackie kicked out in all directions – upset, I daresay, not to have Christie's reassuring presence near. I often wonder whether he could have been suffering from shock in wondering what perhaps the future held in store. That was the last time I saw my uncle.

A week or two later, Christie left Da Skyurds and made his way around the voe (on foot) with his milking pail to milk his young cow and to give her calf his afternoon drink. Seeing as she was still at the kicking stage he had taken her into the byre and tied her in her stall. Quite some time later, Mimie Ellen arrived at Bonhouse asking the workmen whether they had been aware of Christie. She had noticed that neither the cow nor Christie was anywhere to be seen and had assumed he had maybe taken Blackie up for a taste of fresh grass within the Hunshiks yard (which lies up a bit from the house). The workmen had noticed Christie taking his cow into the byre but, as they had been busy at their work, they hadn't taken notice of his movements afterwards. He was discovered lying dead of a massive heart attack in the byre. Mimie Ellen was greatly distressed and so was everyone else.

So Uncle Christie's funeral took place from Da Skyurds. While the men were away at the service in Aith Church, a telegram arrived at Da Skyurds to inform Mimie Ellen that her sister-in-law, Matthew's wife, had died. She had been in hospital for some time so her end wasn't unexpected.

Uncle Christie and Mimie Ellen's Wedding

Uncle Christie and Mimie Ellen's wedding took place in Clousta Schoolroom on 22nd April, 1926, when I was eight years old. I think that the Slyde folk had been thinking he was a confirmed bachelor for by the time he married he was 42. Mimie Ellen would have been aged about 35 at the time of her marriage.

So let me get on to tell you about their wedding. My sister Liza was bridesmaid and Edmund Tait, from Greenmeadow (nephew of the bride), was best man. Those two were quite young compared with the bridal couple. Liza went to Bonhouse in the afternoon of the wedding eve, and early on the day of the wedding some of my brothers and our cousin Peter also proceeded to Clousta.

The transport was across Aith Voe from Slyde to the noost at Stiva. Ertie Moffat from the Gerts in Aith had got what could have been the very first car in Aith, so he had been hired to take the wedding guests by road to Clousta. Sometime during the afternoon it became my turn to get into the rowing boat, then up to the road at Stiva where Ertie awaited us. The boat had to be secured in readiness for the return journey. Being in a motor car was quite a novel experience for John Robert (my nephew) and me, and I don't think our elders had been in cars all that often either. Ertie Moffat's car had a glass partition between the driver and his passengers. Faider sat in the front with Ertie, and I imagine we were a bit out of our element in such circumstances. The memory is still vivid.

There was no road up to the house at Bonhouse, only a cart track from the turning-place down near the school, so we walked up da gaet, past the peat stack and along below the yard daek and up a steep bit till we reached the house.

The first thing that took my eye, on sitting down in the restin chair below the window, was a pair of Japanese pictures hanging on the opposite wall. Mimie Ellen's brother, Freddy Tait, was a merchant navy officer on ships trading out East and over the years he had brought home various ornaments and pictures. Another item of interest was a ship in a bottle. What a marvel! Through time I came to discover how a ship could be put into a bottle. That ornament took pride of place on the middle of the but-end mantelpiece.

Circa 1951: Uncle Christie, Maggie, Madeleine and John Robert, Mimie Ellen. John Robert (author's nephew) and his wife Madeleine whose home was in Ayrshire, would have been in Shetland on holiday. In front are their three eldest children, Robert, Marie and Charlie. Marie came to Slyde for many summers – John Robert really enjoyed having conversations with her in Shetland dialect.

When we arrived at Bonhouse that day the bridal party still hadn't arrived back from the Manse, where the marriage had been solemnised by the Rev. John T. Millar. After tea and homebakes had been devoured, I was taken upstairs along with other females to see all were titivated and to have my hair ribbon tightened up. My hair was so straight and soft a ribbon never stayed in place for long. Liza had a way to tying it so tight it sometimes didn't feel at all comfortable.

After all that, the folk in the house, led by the bride and groom, proceeded down the gaet to the school. I don't remember what sort of eats were served; I only remember the tea being so very hot – John Robert, aged about five, got his cup on the bride's table, shut his eyes and began to blow his breath towards his cup long before his lips made contact. That amused the bride and groom and others sitting near enough to notice, but there was no way muggins was was going to be laughed at!

The iced cake was there on the table, the first cake I had ever seen. I remember quite well that the Clousta postman, Andrew Mitchell, who lived in Twatt, toasted the newlyweds. I don't remember much of what he said, except he ended by saying, "Joys to be multiplied, troubles divided, illnesses subtracted and children added." I can't recall hearing that toast at any marriage since. It could have been Andrew Mitchell's speciality.

I was enthralled by the fiddle music and possibly there could have been a concertina as well. It was also the first time I'd seen people dancing, mostly the auld-fashioned dances. During the evening we were entertained by Andrew Mitchell playing his small set of bagpipes. We children had heard nothing like it before and John Robert decided it could be great for scaring cows out of a corn rig! I wonder? I don't remember so much about our coming back from that wedding but probably we would have been half asleep and tired out after such unusual excitement.

38

Bonhouse

THE old house at Bonhouse was quite a high house and, having been built on a rocky spur, it felt every wind that blew. Maybe that was compensated for by a splendid view. Once upon a time, when everybody used their legs for going places, Bonhouse folk kept an eye on everything that moved. In the but window lay a small pair of binoculars which always got focused on whoever might be on the move. I daresay it was all part of the day's entertainment!

I can well remember all the details of furniture, all through the house. For years there was no porch at all; two steps led up to a stout outer door. How the south-east gale could whistle through the keyhole! At first that eerie noise frightened me until Uncle Christie explained the reason why there was such a noise. In the but-end, which was on the west end of the house, there was a

Bonhouse as it was when I first saw it in 1926

restin chair under the window. It was well padded and covered with some floral material. It made quite a cosy, comfortable seat. In past that was a big wooden arm chair, also padded, with a big cushion and a sheepskin hanging on the back.

The Wellstood American stove was toward the front of the house so it was always warm in that corner; the stove always gave out a good heat. On the other side of the stove stood a big tea box which always held a plentiful supply of peats. Those peats from Stoologue were good quality peat, long and haddy, which means they didn't break easily, nor crumble away into möld. On a winter's day Uncle Christie would come in the door with his kishie towering high with peats which he doosed into the tea box.

The bedroom abune but was kept for visitors. Its door was always kept shut to prevent dust from downstairs entering and spoiling things. That room was always a lightsome place as, besides a skylight, there was a small window set into the west facing gable wall. It was a really thick wall, which gave a deep windowsill where I remember a lovely old-fashioned red geranium seemed to bloom all summer.

Usually there were two beds in that room; a double bed and a single. Both were made up with white sheets and pillow cases trimmed with a broad lace frill. I was fairly enchanted by those fancy pillow cases, for at home we seemed always to have bleached flour bags for pillow slips. For years I slept on pillows covered with those cotton flour bags, still with the brand names of Paul's Best, Millennium or Golden Rod – no amount of sun bleaching or boiling quite erased those names.

Below the skylight stood a long dressing table on which stood photographs and various ornaments, complete with a fair-sized swing mirror in a wooden frame and base. Two or three peerie rugs covered the floor. The chimney had been blocked in – to prevent draughts, I suppose – while a big Japanese firescreen stood in front. More photographs and ornaments were on the mantelpiece. A wooden washstand had a bedroom set consisting of wash basin, ewer, toothbrush holder and soap dish, not forgetting the shanty (chamberpot) standing underneath the lower shelf. Everything was to match and on the side of that washstand there was a rail for towels.

Opening off this room towards the stair, there was another very small room which contained a built-in bed and a chair. A small pane of glass, let into the partition, gave light from the skylight at the top of the stairs, which ascended from the back side of the house.

The ben door was at the foot of the stair. That room, too, was always kept nice – a bed in the corner out past the window was where Betty (Mimie Ellen's mother) usually slept. A round table occupied the middle of the floor, covered with a thick fancy fringed cloth. In winter time there was usually a fire in the tiled grate. A wardrobe with a full length mirror on the door reflected the light from the windows. Many an hour, especially in winter time, I spent looking over all Mimie Ellen's photographs and living out pretence games with my make-believe companions in my make-believe world. Not such a bad occupation at all, when I think back on those times.

Uncle Christie and Mimie Ellen's bedroom was abune ben. Somehow, I never liked that room because there wasn't so much light in it in the summer evenings – not at all what I was used to, a bedroom with a west-facing window.

Almost every day, immediately after dinner before the dishes got washed, the three of them had a short siesta. Betty Doull retired to her bed; Mimie Ellen upstairs to hers, while Christie lounged back in the big basket chair with his cap pulled over his eyes. It was an ongoing habit which went on daily, or at least most days. I usually stayed quiet or went outside.

Betty's younger son, Freddy, I think always had an idea to make his old home at Clousta a more modern dwelling. It had been one of his dreams, though it only materialised in 1952. He had taken note of what a few others had achieved when money became rather more plentiful owing to the Second World War. Many seamen beyond conscription age got steady work during the construction of Scatsta Airport and at the stone quarries at Mavis Grind and North Voxter.

In 1952, Duncan Leask, who had become the tenant of the Skyurds croft, had renovated that old house but hadn't yet moved into it, so suggested that Uncle Christie and Mimie Ellen should flit there while the house at Bonhouse was under renovation. So the workmen had a flitting to do as well.

Captain Tait employed six men to do what proved to be a big job. He was determined not to have a new house built which would have been much easier. The workmen employed were Robbie Leask, Uphoose, Aith; Duncan Leask, Bayview, Aith; Lollie Tait, Hametoon, East Burrafirth; Peter Anderson, Tumblin; Laurie Couper, Setter, Clousta and Jeemie Sandison, Hestataing.

1952: back view of Bonhouse following the renovations.

First they demolished the auld kitchen, the building which joined the old house to the barn and byre. In that building there was a well in the upper corner, referred to as 'da in waal'. It never dried up, and was used for all household purposes except for drinking and cooking (that water had to be carried in enamel buckets from da wast waal which was quite some distance away in the toon o' wast Bonhouse).

Next the roof had to be removed from the old house, shutters set up and adjusted to receive the mixture of cement and sand. You can see from the photo the extension built on the back. There was no such thing as a cement mixer or any of the building aids common today. They carried water for mixing the concrete from another well which lay quite near the back of the old roofless house of wast Bonhouse. It makes one think how buildings got erected all those years ago. All so different from how things are today.

When Uncle Christie died, a telegram was sent to Freddy, who by that time had rejoined his ship. Work on the house came to a standstill until Freddy sent a reply telegram instructing them to carry on and complete what had been started.

39

Next Visits to Clousta

Second visit to Clousta

My second visit to Bonhouse was in January 1927. Mimie, my sister-in law, took John Robert, her younger son George (aged sixteen months) and me across to Clousta for about a week. It would have been around Auld Christmas time in early January. Mimie Ellen dressed John Robert and me as guizers, and took us first down to the Schoolhouse, where at that time a woman named Mary Robertson was living. She sat and laughed at us two peerie trowie tings. From there we were taken to The Grind then up to the Abernethys. Maggie had poodrie straes, which went skidding across the but floor! Poodrie straes were hollow corn stalks filled with a little gunpowder. Once they'd been lit in the hearth they fairly bounced over the floor – primitive entertainment! We had never seen such a thing before. No wonder it sticks in my mind.

By boat to Clousta

My next trip to Clousta took place towards the end of May 1927. This time my brothers Tom and Davie took some of us in a sailing boat all the way by sea. I daresay it was a fine enough day, but one of my memories of that trip was that, when we reached the open sea between Papa Little and Braganess, there was enough swell to make me notice that our house at Slyde tended to disappear from sight for a moment or two when the boat dipped into the trough of a wave. I felt scared, and held on tightly to Liza's hand, but soon we gained shelter from the Isle of Vementry and passed through the narrow waterway of Cribba Sound, which separates the crofts of Uyeasound and Vementry Isle. But soon my fears arose again, when I noticed the black teeth of the Icelanders showing out of the water during ebb tide, with white froth breaking over them; and Maggie Black's Stane seemed a sinister name for a big black stone sticking out of the water to the west of us. I certainly never would have had enough nerve to sail alone around the world! I just wasn't made of the stuff required for such an undertaking. I was relieved to pass Noonsbrough and soon to get ashore at Cumlanoost down below Bonhouse.

I don't know whether we had been expected in Clousta or not but Uncle Christie and Mimie Ellen still hadn't returned from the kirk when we arrived, so Betty was holding the fort.

It's strange how certain details stick in memory. In the old boat house down at Cumlanoost, Liza spied an old boot. Nannie Tait (who at that time would have been courting my elder brother Tom) was with us, so for fun (or was it for good luck?) it was decided to take that old item of footwear up to the house, where it was set on the mantelpiece alongside the ship in a bottle, on top of one of the many fancy tea-tins which were also on the shelf. There was also a pair of gleaming brass candlesticks which sort of caught the eye so that no-one noticed quite a layer of dust covering the lesser objects and nick-nacks of various sorts arrayed along the mantelpiece.

Betty Doull was all in favour of putting the boot on the mantelpiece. She was the sort of person who saw fun in that sort of thing. By and by, Uncle Christie and Mimie Ellen returned from church. Preparations got underway to get food on the table, which got lifted across the room in front of the restin chair under the window. Liza had brought a basket of home-baked bread, etc. so we all sat around the table. My eyes never left Mimie Ellen, wondering how long it might be before she noticed her new ornament. It was only when she got up to pour out more tea that suddenly she began to laugh and said, "Weel, dat is da fairest!" We all laughed – Betty Doull loudest of all!

However, after Liza had helped clear the table and wash up the dishes, it was decided we should go for a walk around the Ness o' Clousta. That was the first of many walks for me in a very special place. I still remember some of the landmarks: da Muckle Head, da Peerie Head and da Mid Head. We went right down to the stone-built saw-pit, in which logs of wood which had come 'wi da sea' got sawn up. Then on to Da Brigs, where a short daek and gate separated the Ness from the Uyeasound property. Up we went to view the rocky tors of

Peerie Bildrin and Muckle Bildrin, then to gaze up the high face of Bret Hamar, and right up the Tap o' Mitchell's Hill – the highest of them all, and from which we could see our home at Slyde lying in the distance away to the eastwards.

I have often wondered who the Mitchell may have been who actually got a rocky hill named after him. Recently I found that Mimie Ellen had a cousin named Mitchell Brown who was born in Clousta in 1835. Perhaps this hill was a favourite haunt of his before he emigrated to Australia in 1856. Anyway, Mitchell's Hill always had significance for me; so much so that I wrote a poem about it. (Appendix 15)

Time fled that lovely summer day, so after teatime we set sail again to make for home. The wind had dropped to just a laar so I had nothing to be scared of really, though when the dipping-lug sail had to be changed around on another tack I held on to the taft with both hands – because a small being, such as I was, might easily have got caught up in the bight of the sail and been swept out to sea! Such are those foolish fears of childhood, though we can only see it that way from an adult point of view.

On the way home it was decided to have a look at the guns which had been erected on Swarback's Head, on the Island of Vementry, during the First World War. From here, all the entrances between Muckle Roe and Papa Little, as well as the Minn, which is the entry to Aith Voe, can be defended. So our peerie boat was left at Northravoe and we had a steep climb from there to where the guns are sited. I wasn't all that impressed when we went into the dark narrow tunnel leading to where the ammunition magazine had been situated. One could never tell what might have jumped out of the darkness, even when, on turning a corner, there appeared a faint glimmer of light. For all I knew it could have been a gunny-man's eyes! I daresay my heart would have been beating overtime!

I was relieved to get back into the boat again. By this time the sea was like glass, the setting sun casting a burnished glow along the surface. Next stop was across to see the Muckle Roe lighthouse. We climbed up steps cut or cemented into the rock face and back down again to where Tom had been keeping the boat safe between the rocks and the cliff face. I felt scared again when Davie climbed the Murbie Stack and came down again carrying his cap containing a few gulls' eggs. I was scared that he might lose his footing and fall between the rockface and the boat. In those days there seemed many things to be scared of, even though I did my best to keep my fears to myself, just in case I got laughed at for being so timid.

40
Holidays at Clousta

HAVING made a few visits to Bonhouse with other family members, I was asked to come across to Clousta for a week or two during the school summer holidays. We must have crossed to Braewick by boat, and Liza accompanied me across the hill from Braewick. She stayed overnight, then left me on my own to fit into an unken house as best I could. After this I spent holidays most years at Bonhouse.

The first evening I think I must have been homesick, for I remember sitting under the yard daek crying to myself while Mimie Ellen and her mother were heaping tatties. Mimie Ellen soon knew what was wrong. She came over to where I sat and spoke kindly then took me into the house and brought out her big box of photographs, which pleased me no end. Maybe it was the fact that Bonhouse was a house from which the evening sun departs early; I had been used to long sunshiny evenings (when the sun was shining) at Slyde where the light from a wide expanse of sea also made everything seem so much lighter. Even today, I am still very much aware of places where evening outstrips shadowy places.

I possessed no toys as such – no books of fairy stories, or a book of any kind, and there were no playmates, as at that time Clousta was very much de-populated. Earlier on in the 19th century there had been maybe fifty children attending school at Clousta. Quite a number came across the hill from Aith, but once Aith got its own school all that changed. The reason for Clousta's depopulation may well have been the lack of a road to Noonsbrough. But before that several families had moved to Lerwick and Leith.

John Abernethy, up at Northouse, was only a month or two older than me but he never came seeking anyone to play with, and Geordie Tait at Flawtoon would have been two years younger. I saw them at the kirk on Sundays but that was all. The only other children were the Henry family at Noonsbrough, and they were younger. Anyway, it would seem I preferred my own company. If I had no-one to play with there was nobody to fight with either, so I was happy in a small imaginary world of my own, always speaking aloud to imaginary folk who never let me down.

Having thought more about all those houses, and of the huge families I discovered from census records of the late 19th and early 20th centuries, I wondered how it had come about that the population had declined so rapidly. I reached the conclusion that the main reason was because there were so many unmarried folk. I don't know the reason why those who had opted to stay on in Clousta had shied clear of wedlock. As a Robertson man living in West Burrafirth once said, when asked why he had never thought to get married, "Well, I can aesy tell dee dat; da desirable wisna obtainable, an da obtainable wisna desirable." I somehow feel sure that attitude may well have ruled the Clousta folk too! Wha's tae say

1904/1905: Matthew Tait is the man in the middle. On the right is the corner of the Clousta hotel; on the skyline is Bonhouse.

41

Some of the People Who Lived in Clousta

Clousta school teachers

I do not know exactly when a school was first opened but it was operational by 1881. William Laurenson from Toft was teacher at Clousta until the Aith School was built and he got the headmaster's job there, in January 1922.

Mary Hunter from Tumblin might have been the next teacher, but I am not certain. Next, I think, came Hannah Henderson, from Papa Stour; Dolly Moncrieff from Weisdale; Emma Umphray from Reawick and Mrs Nellie Manson from Lerwick. I cannot be sure which one of those last three was the very last teacher. Nellie Manson had two young children of school age, named Rose and Jim. I somehow think she went to teach children in Fetlar after leaving Clousta.

Meeting each of them in turn at Bonhouse more than likely makes them stick in my memory, for the simple reason that I was always interested in people – where they came from and who they were related to, etc. The reason I came to meet the teachers was because they usually spent a night or two – or maybe longer – beside Mimie Ellen, before getting their house in order down at the Schoolhouse.

I was also very interested in the names of their boyfriends! All seemed to have a car, which was a step up in those days. On reflection, young folk in those days didn't often change partners; at least three of those young women teachers married the fellows they had teamed up with, even though it may have been a few years until the wedding took place. It was a much more stable society before the Second World War came along, and in my opinion there is no comparison to the instability of today's fast moving masses of young folk.

I see I have departed somewhat from my subject; but those young teachers at Clousta and their boyfriends tried to save some money before they committed themselves to marriage and with hopes to raise a family. I assume those fellows would have turned up latish on, on Friday evenings, to take their girlfriends back to their parents' home. It is most unlikely they ever went out anywhere else. Then on Sunday evenings they would have been brought back to Clousta and so would have been ready for their work on Monday morning. When eventually those couples got married, Uncle Christie and Mimie Ellen always got an invitation to the wedding, and I can remember lots of wedding photographs being received, and later still would come pictures of the children.

The Clousta School closed sometime in the mid-1930s and the few remaining pupils were driven to Twatt School with Edmund Tait from Greenmeadow as their chauffeur. As time moved on, Twatt School got closed too.

Nearest neighbours

The croft known as West Bonhouse was vacant in 1926. Maggie Abernethy was the tenant by the time I remember going to Clousta. As far as I know, Maggie didn't ever stay overnight, but every day she was there attending to her animals and her rigs of cultivation.

Up on the east side of the Bonhouse crofts, the first croft was Geordie Abernethy's. He had never married and lived alone. The Haa was vacant; a Robinson family was the last to live there; the only one of that family I remember was Mary, who came to Quienster as housekeeper sometime around 1927.

You can still see the remains of the old stone-built house immediately on your right as you cross the grid at Da East Grind. That croft was known as Skraefield. I found it uninhabited by the 1881 census. It became amalgamated with the Bonhouse croft sometime later.

Geordie Clocky

At Northouse lived a family of Abernethys and further along, at the Taftlands, there lived a family of Williamsons – Geordie and three sisters. It seems they had all been born on Papa Stour. By the mid-1920s they were middle-aged and none of them had been married.

Geordie Williamson was known locally as Geordie Clocky, owing to the fact he had a flair for repairing pendulum clocks. Folk came from near and far with clocks for Geordie to adjust and mend. At first, I hadn't known why people referred to this man as Geordie Clocky; I thought he either produced clockin hens or, who knows, he might have done a bit of incubating on his own! Such is the imagination of childhood. Mimie Ellen had a good laugh over that.

One day, Mimie Ellen took me along to the Taftlands to collect a clock which Geordie had been mending. It was the only house I was ever in which still had a hearthstone on the middle of the but floor. I never thought anything of it, because I had been to many houses with open fires at the gable wall. I remember a thin film of paet reek lay up over the sooty twartbacks, each couple sporting a sooty tendril while a sooty, reekie smell pervaded everything.

I don't remember much about the so-called furniture, except a few low, wooden chairs and a wooden restin chair, besides wooden chests placed against the walls. On a low table there were several clocks, all ticking away, each at its own pace. I daresay that table would have been Geordie's worktop. He also had a small magnifier and a small bottle of oil into which was stuck a maa's pen – a feather from a gull's wing. I wouldn't know, but I wonder whether they ate their food sitting on chairs around the fire with plates balanced on their knees.

Manse

Across da meadow lay the Church and Manse. At that time the minister was John F. Millar. He was a widower, but he had a sister living with him. She was always referred to as Miss Millar. Beenie Jamieson was their housekeeper. They had a wireless set, the first one in Clousta. I remember Uncle Christie, Mimie Ellen and I being invited to the Manse for supper around a Christmas time. I don't think I enjoyed it much as I was too scared I did the wrong thing by picking up the wrong fork!

Grind

Down below the manse was Da Grind. At the back of that house there was a wooden building which served as a shop. Many a trip I made to that shop for messages, with a small wicker basket with a handle. This shop was really a branch shop from Clark & Co. in Aith. It was run by John Robertson (a brother-in-law to Andrew Clark, who ran the shop in Aith). John lived with his two sisters, Maggie and Mary (none married).

John was a fair and diligent shopman. He was so very painstaking over everything he did. I still remember John weighing out a pound of apples on his old-fashioned weighing scales (with all those various small weights) until all was evenly balanced: first I asked for a pound of apples; John selected the 1lb weight then slowly took the brass scoop across to the box of apples, slowly he selected a few, at the same time reckoning in his mind whether a certain group of apples would weigh anywhere near a pound; next he came back over to the counter where he would discover his calculations had not been entirely correct, so one apple would be exchanged for another. I cannot remember him ever coming across with two apples in his hand and so saving time. But there seemed always any amount of time. It was only me who wanted John to get a wiggle on!

Another task John was most particular about was when he had to measure out a gallon of paraffin oil. There was a barrel of oil laid on its side a little way out from the door of the shop; John had two measuring cans with a flange on one side for pouring the oil through a filler into the customer's paraffin tin; he let the oil flow fast until he knew it was well up his half gallon measure, then he eased off the tap only allowing a slow drip to pass from barrel to jug – not a drop ever got spilt, nor did John ever sell short measure. His method of dribble, dribble, dreep, made everything just right. I wonder whether he may have had a padlock on that paraffin barrel? Probably not; people in those days were pretty honest. Sometimes John's method of getting the basket filled tried my patience, so much so, that I felt like taking over the shop and giving him a kick in his stern.

By watching John, maybe a lesson was learned – always to be fair to everybody. Of course, he was an employee of Clark & Co. so would have been on a weekly wage. I don't remember, as a child, ever getting a sweetie out of his sweetie jars. All had to be accounted for.

John and his sisters had been members of a family of nine; those who had married had moved away from Clousta. They had their croft; Maggie attended the cows and sheep; Mary kept the house in a spotless condition and, of course, both women did a lot of knitting. They all had good singing voices. I think John could also play the fiddle.

1931: Clousta. Back left to right: Ellie Jamieson (Newhouse), Jeannie Moffat (peerie Freddy's other granny), Christie Anderson (Bonhouse), peerie Freddy Tait, Betty Tait (nee Doull – Mam a Bonhouse). Front: Maggie Abernethy, the author, Phemie Tait (peerie Freddy's mother).

Newhouse

Up at the Newhouse (the very first house, quite near the road, as you come in to Clousta) there were Tammie Jamieson, his wife Mimie, and his sister Ellie. Tammie and Mimie had no family. I well remember the time, after I was a mother of four, when I said to Mimie that I'd need to hurry home as I had ironing to do. Her advice was "Lass, du's taen da time ta waash da claes, an' gottin it dry, so whit mair does it need?" She was quite right!

The houses on the way to Noonsbrough

There was no road to Noonsbrough until sometime in the mid-1930s, so the school was still in operation even though there were few pupils. A very good footpath led from the school, past the back of a low thatched-roof dwelling, Da Ayres, and up a steep slope until it sort of levelled off towards Stormytail and on past the door of another thatched house at Crookaness. From there, the path led on towards Pontin. I should think that from there the new road, when laid down, may have followed some of the outlines of that old path.

The old cottage down at Da Ayres lay low in a snug, sheltered corner. It had once been the home of the family of Hughie and Nannie Tait. Two sons, named Jeremiah and Robert, had emigrated to Australia. Another, named Hugh, had been registrar for Sandsting and Aithsting. Anyway, when I first went on holidays to Clousta only the youngest daughter, Willa, was living there; she was unmarried. What I remember most was that there was this fairly big yard in front of the house, filled with gooseberry bushes as well as blackcurrant and wine berries (redcurrants). I was at Willa's house many a time. Mimie Ellen said I shouldn't eat too many berries as Willa needed them for jam making, but she never banned me from eating hers at Bonhouse!

Right across the road from Da Newhouse was Rockytoon, occupied by an elderly couple, Jeemie and Mary Tait. At Crookaness lived Teenie Tait and her sister Baabie. No marriage for either! I was often at Pontin with Mimie Ellen. I remember two old ladies who sat on each side of the fire, always knitting – I think they were sisters and had been closely related to the Flaws family who had once lived at West Bonhouse.

The Skyurds house was vacant and so was the Wart. I think the Jamiesons at Newhouse had tenancy of both those crofts. Up the hill a bit, and around a corner out of sight, lay Flawtoon, a croft occupied by John Tait and his wife Georgina Flaws, with a family of four. They were all older than me, except Geordie. John's sister Nannie also lived there.

Across the Loch of Clingswater lies the croft known as Hjawberg. The last inmate died there in 1917; I believe her surname was Ninianson and that she was burnt. All I remember is a roofless ruin.

At the Loch lived a widow named Nannie (Agnes) Nicolson. Nannie was getting well on in years the first time I was taken to see her. It must have been during my Christmas holidays because Mimie Ellen and her mother had been 'trang kempin' to finish knitting a woollen underskirt for Nannie o' da Loch's Christmas box. I can see it yet, in my mind's eye, blue with a different coloured scallop edge at the hem. What a cosy peerie house Nannie lived in, it seemed to me. A lovely lowin' fire lit up the room and all seemed warm and bright. I suppose she would have had an old age pension, and her relations at Noonsbrough would no doubt have seen to her needs. I can still remember the tears in her eyes on trying to say thank you to Mimie Ellen and her mother for that petticoat which certainly would have helped keep her body warm on a cold winter's night. She sent her blessings to Betty Doull.

I also remember a small house named Da Loch in which lived an elderly woman alone. I don't know whether there was a croft attached, or was it what once was termed an outset.

In those days there were no handouts from a Welfare Trust or whatever. Relations and neighbours kept a watchful eye on anyone living alone, making sure they were never forgotten or neglected, and asking for nothing in return. They knew full well that when any one of them found themselves in like position, the same kindness would be forthcoming to them. When the frailty of extreme age sometimes took its toll, a relation or neighbour would give them refuge within their own home.

But it's time to leave Auld Nannie's and look down at Setter, where there were two occupied houses. In one lived auld Fraser Jamieson and his second wife, Maggie Tait. I think Maggie had been a tall woman for I remember noticing how very bent she was when I saw her walking outside. Trying to figure out why she seemed so doubled up, I asked Mimie what was wrong. Her reply maybe had a ring of truth in it: "Du needna be fairt dat du'll ever geng twafauld, for du'll never growe sae lang as ta bend ower as far as Meggie o' Setter."

In the other Setter house lived young Fraser Jamieson and his wife Meena. Fraser (senior) had been married in his youth to Catherine Dalziel from Stiva, Aith, and had had some family besides young Fraser. Beenie at the Manse and Mimie at da Newhouse were daughters of Auld Fraser. I don't think young Fraser and Meena had any family.

Another thing very vivid in my memory is of Freddy Jamieson from Leith (grandson of Auld Fraser's) coming to Setter during his summer vacation and having his bagpipes with him. More than once I remember, on lovely sunny evenings, Freddy on the knowe abune Doonaberg skirling away on his pipes. Everybody would stand outside their houses and listen. Freddy joined the RAF and went missing on active service in May 1940, aged 27. He had been a pupil at Clousta School before the family moved to Leith.

I think the next croft house was Galdren, where Jeemie lived alone (another bachelor). He would have been middle aged, but what I mind best about Jeemie o' Galdren was how he would also entertain da Clousta folk by taking his wind-up gramophone, with a big green coloured horn, outside on a table. Very often he would choose a sunny evening with a very light wind. Uncle Christie would come and announce, "Galdren is windin' up his hurdy gurdy!" So we all sat out on the rocks 'be wast da hoose' and listened to Harry Lauder singing old songs, as well as Will Fyffe, and Scott Skinner and Neil Gow playing high hornpipes! He usually ended up playing hymns, so he surely pleased aabody. I can also remember, one winter's evening, Jeemie coming by sea across the mouth of the voe with his gramophone and his box of records. Uncle Christie went down to the shore to meet him and to help carry up the records. Woe betide anybody who so much as whispered while Jeemie's records were being played. That would have been an insult.

Here I'll need to leave Jeemie and his gramophone to move from Galdren to Skeotaing. That house was vacant by 1925. It was in that house that James M. S. Tait (lawyer in Lerwick) was born. I think after the old folk passed on then other family members – or at least some of them – emigrated to Australia or New Zealand.

Skeetaplooch was also vacant. It lies in a hollow which, during wet weather, would have been a proper swaarloch.

Next comes Noonsbrough, a very picturesque place. Once there had been at least three crofts at Noonsbrough, but the two outermost were vacant by the time my uncle went to live at Clousta.

The middle croft had been occupied by Magnie Moffat, his wife Jeannie (Tait), and a big family. Most of the sons of the Moffat family had gone into the merchant navy. After Magnie died, in 1918, and some of the daughters married and moved away, things just got too heavy a burden so Magnie Moffat's widow and the remainder of his family decided to move to Lerwick.

Peter Henry and his wife Jessie, who at that time occupied the innermost croft, took over the tenancy of the other two making it a more worthwhile project. Peter and Jessie had a young family and I think his mother, and sister Mary Jane, lived there too. That family derived benefit from the new road and today it's good to see new houses built there in such a peaceful spot.

Everything is so changed nowadays. I sometimes feel that what I remember could be only a dream, but it's not. The biggest drawback in days gone by was that Noonsbrough and the nearby crofts had an extremely hard struggle flitting peats by sea, from a place called Da Vaddils, right at the head of the voe to Unifirth. They had to watch the tide through a narrow tidal waterway between Marlee Loch and the sea. I was never at a flitting there but I heard about it, how the tides ruled the lives of peat-flitters. It took a combined effort of a lot of folk to bring home a firing.

Greenmeadow

The Greenmeadow doesn't lie within Clousta itself, but on its own, midway between Twatt and Clousta. The children from there were pupils at Clousta School and the family attended Clousta Kirk. Mimie Ellen's half-brother John, who had been born at Bonhouse in 1863, was tenant at Greenmeadow when he died, in 1903.

By the time Uncle Christie and Mimie Ellen got married, a new house had been built at Greenmeadow, not far down from the road. Mimie Ellen took me there on a visit to her sister-in-law Betty, two of her unmarried daughters, Beenie and Janet, and her son Edmund, who had a hiring business. Beenie, I assume, kept the house going while Janet did dressmaking; she was also the organist at Clousta Kirk. Betty, their mother, did a lot of outside work, and lived to be an old woman. She died around 1948.

42

The Clousta Hotel, 1896-1907

NOW for some history about a hotel that was once in operation at Clousta. I do not know how such a project really came about, or whose brainchild it was, but in April 1896, an advert appeared in *The Shetland Times* seeking staff to get things under way.

I understand quite a number of young local women were employed as housemaids, table maids, etc. I can't really give any proper details as I only ever heard the Clousta Hotel referred to in a vague sort of way, and I never thought to ask those older people, who would have remembered it all in full swing!

Goodness knows where those guests came from. All would have arrived in Shetland by sea, disembarking either at Lerwick or Walls, from one of the North of Scotland steamships. Surely a gig would have transported them to Clousta. The attractions for tourists in a quiet place like Clousta were fishing, shooting and walking; maybe some came up to our northern isles for health reasons, for rest and fresh air.

There was an abundance of trout in all the lochs round about the Clousta area, and boys of school age earned twartree pennies acting as gillies. Also people would have gone off-shore with a handline to catch haddock or whiting.

From the photograph (overleaf) you will get some idea of the size of the Clousta Hotel and where it was sited – quite near the shore at the head of the voe. You can see the window and craa-head of the schoolhouse on the right hand side of the picture.

Clousta Hotel.

One wonders whether it was really a paying project or not. It did give some employment and, more than likely, local crofters would have found a handy outlet for milk, butter and eggs, and maybe a bit of mutton too. I wouldn't know whether hosiery would have been sold to those tourists. At the turn of last century folk in Shetland were very poor, though I daresay there were always those who had a ready aptitude to 'turn ower a penny an mak twa'.

The Clousta Hotel was a wooden building with concrete gables. Early one morning, around September 1907, the whole establishment went up in flames. The fire was thought to have started in the kitchen, and, of course, there were those who hinted that the fire may have been started wilfully, as the whole concern wasn't making a profit, and the only way to recoup expenses would have been to claim on fire insurance.

I do not know the whole story, nor all the whys and wherefores. I can only remember part of a gable, including a chimney, which stood for many years as a sad reminder of its former glory!

I recall Betty Doull telling that on the morning of the fire she had decided to take a cow to a roup at Sandwater, and how she had had to take a wide detour into da meadow to get clear of the smoke and flames. Somehow, I got the impression that Betty wasn't really sorry to see the end of the hotel: "Dey joost set da kye mad wi dir shuttin, an' trampit trow da cuttin girse."

43

Andrew Matthew Tait (1887-1969)

I CAN'T leave Clousta without mentioning Mimie Ellen's two brothers, who I got to know when they returned to live in Bonhouse, in 1952.

Mimie Ellen's elder brother was Andrew Matthew. His mother always referred to him by both names, though to everybody else he was known as Matthew. We only came to get acquainted with Matthew after he retired and came to live at Bonhouse after the old house got renovated.

One Christmas Day, when Matthew was 12 or 13 years old, he and some of his pals thought to act grown up and fire some shots from a gun, as that was part of the celebrations in those days. I don't know exactly what sort of a firearm this would have been. I know nothing of guns except that they are dangerous weapons and not to be played around with. How it actually happened I do not know, for there were others involved in quite a dangerous ploy, but it ended with the thumb of Matthew's right hand being blown off. He grabbed a towel and managed to wrap it around the wounded hand as tight as ever he could, and made off as fast as he could run up to the Newhouse, where at that time Dr James Bowie was in residence (before Parkhall got erected). Matthew's mother, very upset, was close on his heels, while the other boys who had been present when the accident occurred followed close behind. When Matthew told me of that day, he laughed, and said, "We must have looked like the Pied Piper of Hamelin!"

On leaving school he got employment at Clousta Hotel, and would have been nearing his 20th birthday by the time it got burned down. He accepted the manager's offer to come south to Glasgow and he worked in The Imperial Hotel until he retired. By then he had been keeping tabs on three hotel bars.

Often, he had to act as bouncer, and although Matthew was not a tall man he soon had rowdy clients out the door, by pushing the bony joint end, where his thumb had once been attached, into the back of their necks. "That made them think I was using a pistol!"

During the First World War, Matthew joined the Army and was soon posted to France. I am not certain in what regiment he served, but I think he may have been in the catering department as I know he was never in the trenches. He and others were accommodated in some sort of barracks in which there were double bunk beds; at night there was always a competition to see who could kill the greatest number of rats by dropping a bayonet from the upper bunks. Listening to that true story made me shudder.

Another experience he told of was the day he and one of his mates, while out for a walk in France, came upon a farm where there was a large flock of hens scratching about. Thinking this would be a good place to procure some eggs they approached the farmer's wife. Not being able to speak French, and because the woman couldn't understand a word of English, they tried to make themselves understood by crouching down with arms outstretched and moving them up and down like hens' wings, all the while making clucking noises. But the woman didn't catch on at all, and seemed puzzled as to what they wanted. Anyway, it ended by her showing them into a very primitive toilet! They, of course, had a good laugh over that.

Eventually Matthew decided to draw eggs on a scrap of paper and in the end they got through to the woman what all their

Matthew Tait and his wife, Margaret.

antics had really been about. From then on they made a point of going along there whenever they were short of eggs.

I used to wonder whether the deaths of his wife and brother-in-law (Uncle Christie) within a few days of each other may have been the deciding factor for Matthew giving up his home in Glasgow and moving back to Bonhouse. I should have asked him, but somehow only came to think about it when it was too late. Maybe he came for Mimie Ellen's sake, to help her settle back at the new house at Bonhouse.

Matthew was of a very pleasant disposition, with a ready wit. From 1960 to 1970, Jeemie and I had the sub-let of the croft at Bonhouse. For most of that time Matthew lived alone. I can never remember going there and finding him in a black mood; sometimes he needed some small item mended, or maybe he was just glad of our company. Often, he would greet us with, "You've come as an answer to a maiden's prayer." We felt sorry for him, an auld lonely body, with only his memories of a very busy life away down in Glasgow.

Matthew was not interested in genealogy and had never given a thought as to who was the old man, Anton Doull, who died at Bonhouse, in 1898. Once, I remember, when speaking of old times, he said, "And who was Anton?"

"Good grief! He was your grandfather," said I, who was always interested in who was related to who. Perhaps he had been too young to understand the relationship.

Through time, the ageing process took its toll. He was eventually admitted to Montfield Hospital where he passed away on 6th October, 1969.

Frederick Bowie Tait (1893-1958)

MIMIE Ellen's younger brother Freddy Tait, had, like many other young men in Shetland, chosen the merchant navy as his career and ended sailing as captain on some of the Ben Line ships. He saw active service in both world wars. He had made his home, after his marriage in 1925 (to Phemie Moffat), at Breiwick Road in Lerwick, where their son, also Freddy, was born. Phemie died around 1943.

Freddy Tait married a second time, to Maggie Robertson from Grind, Clousta, around 1949, and she accompanied him on a voyage to Australia where she met again

Freddy Tait and his first wife, Phemie (Euphemia, née Moffat).

her eldest sister (Martha), who had married many years earlier and settled there.

Captain Freddy Tait gave up his seafaring around 1953, gave up his house in Lerwick, and he and Maggie also moved into the Bonhouse house. From my point of view it could never have been a satisfactory set up. Four elderly folk, who had lived quite different lifestyles apart from each other, must have found it extremely difficult to fit in together. However, that situation only lasted a few years.

When Freddy retired from his seafaring career, he stood unopposed for Aithsting as county councillor and served from about 1954 up to the time of his sudden death, in October 1958, aged 65. His wife died only three months later, so that left Mimie Ellen and Matthew together.

Section 7

Transport

The Voe to Aith Road

WE, of the oldest generation alive today, ask each other, "Can du mind?" It's then we all feel how much we have missed by failing to ask those who were old when we were young. Much has been lost by failing to do so.

I do not know exactly when the Voe to Aith road was first laid, but from snippets heard years ago, I would say it happened between 1910 and 1912. Men came from a wide area to work on this stretch of road; one gang started at the Voe end while others began at Aith. I imagine the road from Bixter to Aithsness had been laid earlier, but I have no way of knowing that.

We used to wonder how it was that the road bypassed the township of East Burrafirth and were told that those elderly Tait men, who occupied the crofts near the head of East Burrafirth Voe, had a conflab under the gable of one of their houses: "We don't need any road; we hae boats an' legs which can tak wis ony wye we want ta go," they agreed. Another factor in those days was that they felt the whole place would be laid open to hill sheep, and cows and horses as well. They won that debate anyway, and East Burrafirth had a long wait before a road was laid.

I do know that by spring 1911 the road from the Aith side came to a near standstill for a time, somewhere near Da Klaaber Knowes, on the rise before descending towards Meena's Brig (the bridge spanning Lunklet Burn where you leave the road to walk up to Ramnahöl, the waterfall made famous by the photograph taken by Dennis Coutts). Perhaps the road there had been held up owing to the building of Meena's Brig or maybe that could have been where the final link up was made. I have no idea, and nobody I have asked can enlighten me as to where it joined up, or the date. I don't suppose there would have been such a thing as an opening ceremony.

I understand there were two Ratter men from Hamar, Northmavine, masons by trade, who were responsible for the bridge building; both had an eye for precision (when building a stack of peats they kept a big sharp knife handy so as to cut off any offending projections!)

Most of the workmen who didn't live in the vicinity got lodgings in houses round about. That was how Jonathan Tulloch, from Bardister in Northmavine, met Baabie Abernethy of Winnaness.

I have no way of knowing whether the road-making work was carried on right through the dead of winter or not. Certainly it would have been held up in snowy weather. They surely would have had some sort of shelters built in which to eat their grub. No vacuum flasks in those days so they must have had peats to make a fire on which to boil a tea kettle. I remember the foundations of a roddy-man's house in Briggidale, half way down the stretch of road between the Muckle Knowe and the Peerie Brig. I have been told that this house was of fair size; there were plenty of moorie faels to be had, a moorie bench on each side could be used as a settee or a bed on which to sleep. A sack packed with heather made a good mattress. No doubt bits of wood 'come wi da sea' would have been used as couples over which flaas could have made a waterproof roof. And if a leak happened to drip, who cared? There was a plentiful supply of flaas handy to make a roof watertight – nobody was house-proud in those days.

(Flaas were riven (torn) by hand from certain heathery areas of the hill, preferably young heather. A man stood, legs wide apart, stretching forward as far as he could reach. With arms outstretched he sort of loosened the heather roots with both hands on three sides then pulled the narrow loose edge towards his feet, ending up with a heather rug affair. I imagine a tall man with long arms could have riven quite some flaa! The heather had to be pulled against the grain and a note had to be taken of the state of the tide! Flaas, like many another job around the croft, could only be riven on a flood tide! They were left to dry on the hill for a week or two then tied with coir rope and carried home. Flaas were used even in my youth for covering lambhouse roofs. They 'sembled tagedder' better than poans and resisted storms. (Poans – lubba grass dug with a spade as shallowly as possible; used to cover potatoes as they were easily opened.)

Starting at the Voe end, first a bridge had to be built over da Burn o' Kirkhouse, then up a nasty, steep brae where the ravine of Kringigyill had to be crossed, before ascending further to Gonfirth Loch where the hard rock face had to be tackled. There must have been some sort of gelignite used here, as I imagine the side of the hill would have been sheer into the loch.

From Gonfirth Loch the road rises to 360 feet above sea level, one of the highest roads in Shetland. On a clear day a superb view takes in all the hills to the westward, with Foula and the Vee Skerries clearly visible. The youngsters of today seem to call this the Alps, which they say is as apt a description as any. If you chance to be driving over that special bit of road on a clear evening during the hours of darkness, stop your car, get out, and you will see something twinkling away in the distance. If you have a pair of binoculars use them, and you will see the lights on Papa Stour!

Next the road bends and descends past the end of the Grobsness road (built in the 1930s) and down over the Gonfirth Brig. Another rise followed by a dip down the Brae o' Sudderhouse, before another bend and a sharp corner at the Methodist Chapel of Gonfirth.

The Unseen Stores lay below the road, and Gonfirth School near the road on the left. A short level bit takes us to da Brig o' Voxter, before again ascending a long slope until you reach da Muckle Knowe. Near here, almost at the top of the brae, the road passes between Delting and Aithsting. There's no marker to say so, but that's where it is.

Once past da Muckle Knowe you come to Briggidale from where the road leads down to East Burrafirth. I understand that part of that stretch of road was termed a floating road – that is, it had no firm rock foundation. Apparently those versatile flaas were just laid down, heathery side lowermost, and covered with mortar taken from a small quarry at da Muckle Knowe. It would have packed together solid enough by rain and the trampling of men's big boots. That piece of road used to undulate in waves after a heavy truck had passed over.

Past da Peerie Brig and still down, down until you reach Meena's Brig, the mother of them all. Thereafter the road winds along the east side of Aith Voe. At the foot of Aith Manse brae there is a bridge over Wirlie Burn, and nearer the Aith/Vementry crossroads another brig spans a slow flowing burn, named da Mill Burn because there used to be a water mill there almost down at the sea. At da Shippin Office corner the road goes in to Vementry and out to Bixter. Before cars became common, it was a favourite place for the young people to gather and chat, especially after the church service, before heading homewards in different directions. Seeing the youngsters gathered there reminded one of the older seamen of sailors gathering round Shipping Offices when they looked for work.

Around 1960 the whole of the Voe to Aith road got a good surface of tarmacadam, in time for the queen to travel in comfort from Aith to Voe. It was not always so. Heavy rains and frosts played havoc with those old mortar roads and when the odd car passed over them in dry weather they raised clouds of dust. So each small gang of roddy-men was kept busy the whole year mending pot holes and cracks, besides the clearing of choked cross-drains. Those roddy-men of years gone by were famed for taking their time over any small maintenance job; they always seemed to have the time to light up their pipes and rest on their shovels, ever ready for a chat with anyone who happened to pass; and sometimes the passers-by were many, for almost everybody travelled on foot.

Quite a number of gates crossed the road and although they were essential for keeping out livestock they were a nuisance to other road users.

The Voe to Aith road was, indeed, a dangerous and tortuous road for many years after being laid, and even today, with all its upgrading and smooth surface, is still an awkward highway. But I shouldn't think anyone driving at speed in flash cars would ever give a thought to those workmen all those years ago who toiled to get a road made on very low pay and with little comfort – no working tools except a pick, shovel and wheel-barrows. Plenty of muscle power would have been needed to lift and carry bigger stones for bridge building purposes.

Selkieburn Boatman

John Tait – Johnnie o' Selkieburn (1852-1932)

Before there was a road into East Burrafirth, the most common route to get to the nearest road – the one between Aith and Voe – was by rowing boat, usually to Selkieburn where there is good shelter. This would not be so easy nowadays with the mussel farm at the head of the voe.

At Selkieburn, Johnnie Tait had a peerie blue boat which was often used to transport folk across the mouth of East Burrafirth Voe. Johnnie just kept digging the oars into the water, just enough to keep the boat moving forward in the right direction. The idea seemed to be his way of having time to gather as much local gossip as he could on the journey across! I imagine his passengers would have been 'ower blyde' of the chance to rest their weary legs.

Sometimes, so I was told, young folk from East Burrafirth thought nothing of taking a loan of Johnnie's peerie blue boat in the middle of the night when returning from a box social and dance in the Nort Store at Gudataing. It seems to have been the accepted thing to do.

Johnnie Tait was a very mild-tempered man but apparently was a very light sleeper and more than likely was always well aware of the movements of those youths from Burrafirth out on a spree. He never forgot he had once been young himself, and he is said to have been forever opening his skylight during the silent watches of night. When aware that his boat was being used, he would shout, "Put her back! Put her back!" In those times of long ago, a wife and a boat were said to be a man's most treasured possessions, which he wasn't willing to share with anyone else! Fortunately, next evening the boat would have been put back and Johnnie would have got his dram (and an update on the gossip fae da night afore?).

The safety of that peerie boat depended on who was in charge; maybe there would have been times when 'Johnnie Walker' could have been on board; or maybe just one or two women needing to get to the other side. Anyway, on one occasion, those fellow-me-lads had been careless, maybe not making certain that the boat had been hauled above the high water mark, or neglecting to tie it securely, but in the morning, Johnnie, on looking out his skylight, saw no signs of his boat anywhere. An extra high tide with a gale of wind had lifted the boat and set her on her way, causing her to come to rest on the soft sand just below da Hoit. (Luckily the ert of wind had blown her up to the burn mouth rather than out into Aith Voe, where it might have been the end of her.) Johnnie set off, walking to where she lay, and with help from the Hoit folk he made his boat secure. Never a word of reproach was spoken, for he knew his boat would be put back safely to her noost under the cover of darkness. I have no doubt he would have licked his lips at the thought of a taste from a hip flask or, more than likely, it would have been straight from the bottle!

Johnnie Tait taught all his sons to swim while they were very young; he took them down to the pier at high tide and tied a rope around their waist, which would have given them confidence. That decision stemmed from when, as a young man, Johnnie had fallen overboard from a sailing ship and spent 17 hours in the waters of the Pacific before being picked up.

He passed away in November 1932, aged 80, leaving a good memory to all who knew him. All those young fellows of whom I write have also long gone to rest. Time passes swiftly by, much faster than we are fully aware of. We from East Burrafirth are thankful to have memories worth holding on to now that we have reached the sunset years of life.

Our Road – At Last

1937 – the start

The East Burrafirth folk had a long wait for their road; but at long last, after many disappointments, a notice actually appeared in *The Shetland Times* for tenders to build a road to open up our isolated district. That notice appeared sometime in the spring of 1937 and, as far as I can remember, work began maybe in May or June. Imagine anything happening so fast these days! That was the summer I spent six weeks at Skoes, Sandsound, under quarantine, after having been in contact with scarlet fever. By the time I was allowed back home the road builders were working on the bridge which spans the Mill burn.

The workers

The man who got the contract was a man from North Roe. His name was Jeemie Johnson. He brought with him four youths from Eshaness – Frankie Anderson, Laurie Anderson, Geordie Manson and Willie Johnson. Some local men were also employed – Tammie Hunter (Selkieburn), Tammie Tait (Roadside), Alec Tait (Hoit), Lollie Tait (Hametoon), Robbie Anderson (Slyde), Jeemie Eunson (Skeetalea) and Laurie Couper (Cole). I think Johnnie Nicolson (Scarvataing) may have been on the job too.

I have been told they were paid sixpence an hour, but as there was next to no employment in Shetland during those lean years even a poorly paid job was better than nothing. Most able-bodied men were in the Merchant Navy and when they came ashore to spend a few months at home they went on the dole, but that didn't amount to much. Of course, all the road work had to be done using quarry pick and shovel with a hand barrow and wheelbarrow by way of transport.

Accommodation for the workers

Those fellows from Northmavine got a roof over their heads in the Nort End at Hestataing, which for a few years had been the abode of auld Ertie Moffat. But he had been taken across to his brother's house at da Gerts in 1936. How five men managed to stretch out for a night's rest in so small a space, I do not know. I suppose each would have brought his sack of straw, a pillow perhaps, and a blanket. At that time the only furniture in da Nort End was a small Victoress stove. A plank of wood across two boxes would have made a bench to sit on. The Nort End, at that time, had a door opening outside. There still hadn't been a door taken out between that building and the main dwelling house where the Sandison family lived.

I do not know, but I expect those roddy-men would have been supplied with peat for their stove and milk for their tea. They went home to Northmavine over the weekends where they would have enjoyed better conditions and had at least some home comforts.

Laying the road

Anyway, I will need to make an effort to fill in at least some of the detail concerning the actual laying of that short stretch of road which meant such a lot to everybody in East Burrafirth, especially to us who lived at the far end. Each section got its own name. The steepish slope where East Burrafirth road joins the Voe/Aith road was named Blaandy Brae, from the fact that most of the men came armed with a bottle of whey fortified with a spoonful of oatmeal. Its purpose was to quench thirst, for the work was hard and sometimes the sun was hot.

The local men, especially those who hoped to benefit from the road, were in great haste to see the job done before winter overtook them. One old man, who had been keeping his eye on them, remarked: "Dir no wirkin like roddy-men; dir mair lik mad men!" A bridge had to be built over the small burn which ran down between da Hoit and da Punds. The next part was quite boggy and was soon named da Punds Puddle. After that, quite a deep cut had to be made in solid rock, which got named Culebra Cut by one of the men who, in his seafaring days, had sailed through the Panama Canal.

Later on, as work progressed, it was discovered that the foreman sometimes planted a bottle of cheap beer or red–biddy (I think this was perhaps port wine) down a rabbit burrow. That could well have been an incentive for those sweating labourers to push on. He who happened to be nearest where that refreshment lay hidden might have been in luck. It certainly would have been a change from the sharp taste of blaand!

At our house I remember special containers into which whey was poured after a churning had been done. Seldom did workers of long ago ever go out to do the hard work in the fields without a small pail of blaand.

I expect the kye would have been upset by all the unusual noise and activity. Men working together tended to shout to each other, having become accustomed to that way of speaking in seafaring days. Those on deck had need to raise their voices so as to be heard by those up aloft among the rigging!

I can well remember the walls of a disused mill, just above where the Mill Brig is now. Not a trace remains now. Stones from which that old mill had been built were taken to build the bridge. A road meant much more than the preservation of an old mill. Maybe Rosie, the Hametoon mare, would have missed the shelter it gave on a wet, stormy evening.

1934: carting sheaves at the Hametoon. Left to right: Mootie Tait with Rosie, Mary Tait, Maggie Christie (nee Tait), Laura Tait (Hametoon), Robbie Anderson (Slyde). Rosie would have missed the shelter given by the mill which was demolished to help with the construction of the East Burrafirth road.

Cash shortfall

It was intended that the road would run nearer to the Wasthoose and Holm before going around the hill to Slyde, but money was running short so the end of the road followed the shortest straightest line, and ended at the grind, a good bit up from Slyde. Money did run out before the road got finished, so toward the end Jeemie Johnson, who had bought an old boat, paid those road builders with fencing posts made from the sawn up boat. I daresay that arrangement would have been quite acceptable, for with a new road splitting up crofts there was an urgent need for fences to be erected on both sides of the road. Money was gey scarce in the 1930s, so in-kind payment was often acceptable instead of hard cash.

What a difference a road makes

I still remember how elated we all felt one afternoon in early October, when we actually beheld the foreman's peerie black car on the turning place just outside our Sooth Grind. Mind you, our house at Slyde was still about a quarter of a mile from the road end, but that didn't matter at all. We now had a road. We felt over the moon!

It meant an end to having to carry kishies of peats quite some distance from up on the Nort Hill, and, much more so it meant an end to having to depend on all heavy goods, including paraffin, being transported by sea and carried up the steep path to the house.

Now we had a road. That in itself lightened our load. Grocery vans appeared at our road end. A wheelbarrow was used to transport the goods down to the house. The Nort Hill was abandoned and we, like all the other households in Burrafirth, took up peat banks at Briggidale. The peat moor was poorer quality. As it is a low-lying place sheltered from most erts of wind in a wet summer those lower banks were slow at drying. Heavy, half-dry peats often had to be carried up to the side of the road in the hope that a wind might sift through the long low 'bings' of peat. Later, a lorry was hired and a gang of workers (neighbours) was brought in to help get those peats home, while at least two folk had to stand by to build a stack. It was all hard work, but everybody did what they could to help each other, and much good humoured banter went on among the young folk (and among the older folk too). It could be a really lightsome way to get a heavy job done.

As my memory takes me back over the years it makes me wish I had at least some of the energy which used to be mine. But I daresay that's a foolish wish –

> Noo youth has geen;
> an age haes come;
> nae langer im I a chick!
> A tired heart is wearin dön;
> a battery maks it tick!

That's how it is; it doesn't need much energy to push a pen.

As far as I can remember, a road wide enough to take a car down to the house at Slyde didn't materialise until the 1960s.

The finished road

After heavy rain the surface, in places, became extremely sticky and soft, owing to clay being used for the final surface layer. Clay looked all right while the weather stayed dry, but once a heavy shower of rain came down it became as sticky as one of those old-fashioned fly catchers.

Getting stuck on the road

I can remember one time we were returning home from a wedding in Aith Hall when some of us had to get out and push the car through! Looking out the back window of the car I noticed Johnnie and Mootie Henry just behind us on a motor bike. Both had their feet on the road pushing the bike through da Pund's Puddle. In memory, I see them still. Owing to the motor cycle's head lamps, the scene resembled a huge insect crawling out of a bog!

Aftercare

I think one or two local men, and maybe some older boys, took shovels and wheelbarrows and collected stones and mortar in an effort to reinforce the surface of our highway. Lots and lots of patching up needed to be done later by the regular roddy-men employed by Zetland County Council. Through time, of course, that road was upgraded by getting a fine, smooth surface of tar macadam, so that today it's just as good as any other.

48
Learning to Ride a Bicycle

Bairns nowadays seemingly learn to ride a bicycle fairly young, but I had no chance of that. Living at such an 'oot o' da wye' place like Slyde, with no road, shanks pony was by far the most reliable method for getting to and from wherever we wanted to go.

My brothers and cousin all rode bicycles. Sometimes one would bring their cycle by sea to Slyde, carry it up from the pier on their shoulder, take it in onto the but floor, where they would fiddle away, adjusting, oiling, and maybe fitting a new tube and tyre. More often, perhaps the old one had to be patched. We younger bairns were then allowed to spin the wheels around.

Those cycles the older boys possessed (maybe they just had one between them) got shelter in the barn at Selkieburn or at Hestataing as, of course, any of those fellows wishing to go somewhere with the bicycle first had to make a sea crossing from the Holm or Wasthoose noost, across to the other side – usually in a small skyiff. Now and again, whichever one had been using the cycle would be sure to call along Johnnie Tait, at Selkieburn, or Ertie Moffat, at Hestataing, and give him a good swig from a half bottle of whisky (or whatever). That gesture would have been in appreciation for their kindness in offering shelter to the old bone-shaker.

But once we got a road, the idea presented itself that it would be a good thing to get a bicycle. I can't recall how the second-hand machine was procured, or where it came from, or who paid a few pounds for it. I expect it may have been my father. Anyway, it was sort of a 'halfers' affair between my niece Jean (Robbie and Mimie's daughter) and myself.

Strange as it might seem, the place where I actually got the hang of how to ride a push bike was not anywhere near East Burrafirth, but down the steepish brae – untarred – leading from the crossroads at Gruting down towards the school. It was a splendid feeling!

It came about in this way. In early August 1938, I had gone across to Mootie and Jeemie Johnston at Seaside Cottage, Bridge of Walls, as a loblolly lass to Mootie, not long after her daughter Betty had been born. (Mootie had been born and brought up at the Hametoon in East Burrafirth.) I had become acquainted with her neighbours, Maggie Ann and Ruby Johnston, up at West Houlland. They had a bicycle and one sunshiny evening Ruby decided she would take me to a place where I couldn't fail to learn to balance the bicycle and maybe get the hang of things without falling off and breaking some bones. So … I got my right foot onto the right pedal while my left leg sort of hung limp alongside. Ruby shouted, "Pit up dee fit, lass," but all I could do was get my knee onto the left side pedal.

"Noo, watch whit du's doing; dunna run ower fast; mind it's da back brake du pits on when too much speed mounts up; du'll go head first ower da handlebar if du pits on da front brake; watch oot fir da ruts in da rodd; keep da cycle under control!" I'm sure Ruby couldn't have been far behind and more than likely had a laugh to herself at my first wobbly attempts. That summer's evening remains vivid in my memory.

Yes, of course, I still had a lot to learn when I did get a bicycle of my own at Slyde: how to balance the thing and to work my feet on the pedals at the same time, like other folk could do! Thinking back over all those years its a wonder I didn't break my neck, I had quite a few nasty spills, all of which happened owing to my own ignorance of how much speed a cycle could gather going down a steep brae.

Cycling too fast!

One afternoon, while still at the learning stage (do you ever really leave it?) – by then I could sit in the saddle and use the pedals at the same time – I went down the Wasthoose Brae at quite a lick. Somehow, I lost control in trying to round a sharpish bend at the foot of the brae and the cycle got in among a lot of loose gravel etc. which had washed down the brae during heavy rain. Of course, I came off at full tilt, the palms of both hands were raw and embedded with sand and my shoulder got a nasty rap as well. So I had to endure sore hands for almost a week. "Lass! Whit wis du doin?" etc., etc.

There were so many deep ruts in our new road that it was not an ideal place for any cyclist, let alone a greenhorn such as I. Nothing teaches as experience does, though often it proves to be a hard taskmaster. Another damp evening I did myself a worse misanter by yet another foolish mistake. This time I hadn't had a chance to gather speed, as I was pedalling along from the Wasthoose grind to our one, and on coming down the brae approaching the turntable I discovered that, on applying the brakes, nothing happened, owing to wet wheels and well worn brake blocks. Without any sensible thought, I just held her going right across a deepish drain and on to a heap of stones on the broo at the other side.

I immediately discovered my foolish mistake. I went head first over the handlebars and the cycle did a somersault as well. It was the only time in my life that I actually saw stars! However, no bones were broken, but I sustained a cut or two high up on my forehead. I remember being dismayed to discover that the front forks of the cycle were all askew and quite rigid. It took me some time to wheel my machine on the back wheel down to our house. I daresay I would have been in a state of mild shock, though in those far back days I scarcely knew what the word meant.

It was pretty late that rainy May evening, so although some of our household still hadn't gone to bed, I wasn't too keen on letting on about what had happened. After somehow getting the cycle into the washhouse where it was kept, I became aware of blood trickling down the side of my face so I took a hanky and tried to clean up as best I could. I crept up to bed without showing myself. No lamps were ever lit during the summer months so I managed to escape upstairs without anyone taking any notice of the state I was in. I wasn't at all concerned about myself but I was really worried what might be said when the bicycle had to be brought forth.

I got quite a shock next morning, when on taking a skite into the small mirror I beheld a white face, with quite a large bump on its forehead, besides a proper keeker of a black eye! On going downstairs I was asked, "Whit's happened ta dee? Whit's du been doin' on dat cycle? Du'll brak dee neck yet," etc. At that moment, I'm sure our Auntie Ellen had come to think that getting a road was maybe going to prove a mixed blessing.

My brother Robbie got that cycle fixed up again with a word of advice and warning that one needed to be very careful, and how to act in an emergency. I think I had learned my lesson, so that my pushbike and me got along okay for years after that. Although I haven't ridden a bicycle for many years, I imagine I would manage alright except for the fact that my knees might protest. So, it's all just a memory; but memories are precious.

Cycling in Unst

With Annie Sandison, my future sister-in-law, I spent two weeks at Westing in Unst in September 1941. At that time one of Jeemie's other sisters, Mary, was teaching at Westing. We took our bicycles with us, having sent them to Lerwick on a North of Scotland lorry. We went by car to Lerwick and boarded the *Earl of Zetland* at 8am next morning. I enjoyed the trip north. The *Earl* called at Symbister (Whalsay), Skerries, Brough Lodge (Fetlar) and Mid Yell, before heading north to Unst. We were taken ashore from the *Earl* at Uyeasound by flit boat. Mary met us and we cycled up from Uyeasound to Westing.

In lovely sunshiny weather we cycled all over Unst – trips still vivid in my memory. We, of course, returned on the *Earl* so it would have been late afternoon by the time we reached Lerwick. Leaving our suitcases at the Steamer's Store we cycled all the way home before darkness fell (about 22 miles). I seem to remember a full moon lighted our last few miles from Bixter to Hestataing. Jeemie perhaps escorted me home to Slyde. But at times my memory lets me down!

49

Driving

BEFORE we married Jeemie had a motorbike, so I was often his passenger but was never in command!

January 1940: George Anderson (Slyde) and Jeemie Sandison (Hestataing) with Jeemie's motorcycle.

I was never that keen to try driving. However, one evening in the summer about 1960, coming out from Clousta, Jeemie said, "Whit aboot haein a go taakin da car hame?" I seemed to manage until I reached the road junction at Twatt (driving up hill to a T-junction). Now, whether I hadn't eased my foot from the accelerator, or whether I hadn't turned the steering wheel properly, I don't know, but I ended up careering across the road and managed to splinter three fencing posts!

So ended my driving lesson. "Du soodna spaek sae much; bit try ta concentrate more on whit du's doin." I did manage to move our peerie tractor to and fro on the croft, but I never did drive a car, so now I don't miss it – like I might have done if I had actually turned out to be a road hog.

Section 8

Places to Meet

50
Roups

ROUPS were held twice a year where crofters sold cattle; I guess the last roup would have been in the 1950s. We usually went to Voe where the roups were held in a natural amphitheatre half way up the road which leads from the pierhead towards the Loch of Voe. Other roups within walking distance were held at Sandwater and Bridge of Walls. Auctioneers were often good entertainers. I remember one elderly lady leading her animal around the ring when the auctioneer called: "Gyit on wi da biddin – it's da coo yir biddin on, no da wife!"

In the early 1930s, I remember George and I being sent with a young calf which had never been on a tether before. Instead of a halter, Auntie Ellen, who usually cared for him, had put a rope round his neck. He was a stubborn beast and not acquaint with either of us, so I pulled and George urged him forwards from behind. We struggled along till the calf became aware of the Gonfirth cattle, when he set off at top speed – with only a rope round his neck I had little control. Using one of the laces from my shoes, one of the Gonfirth men made him a halter so we managed better after that. I managed fine with the shoes as we split the remaining lace between the two.

Cash was paid for the cattle; the transaction took place in Adie's office in Voe. Nine pounds for a year old ox was a good price. Tea and sandwiches were sold from one of Adie's sheds and there was the shop to visit too. Not everyone there had an animal to sell – for many it was a social occasion and several marriages followed meetings at a roup.

Voe roups were usually followed by a dance in the old hall which was down by the shore. We took our frocks and dancing shoes with us and got changed at the old manse, where friends lived, before walking along the seashore to the hall. There was no admission charge but we had to pay for supper of tea and bannocks etc. By the time the dance finished the blackbirds were singing. One of the hirers from Aith would be there and as many people as possible piled in to the vehicle for the homeward journey.

51

Cole Dances

TWO or three dances were held at Cole each winter, usually at Aald Christmas, Aald New'rday and in February. News of these dances was by word of mouth or by invitation. The women took cake and the men drink, and the fiddlers were usually Jeemie Balfour or Willie Anderson. Sometimes the men hid the bottles they'd bought for the dance in rabbit holes so that the elders of the household wouldn't know how much drink they were going with. Entertainment was such a rarity; we looked forward so much to these dances and were always concerned that the weather would stop us getting there.

I was 16 when I went the first time. Mootie o' da Hametoon had asked me to go with her. Auntie Ellen tried to dissuade me: "Wait an geng tae a right dance." In the end I set off to the Hametoon carrying my knitting and wearing a frock with a peenie over it; she thought I was going to stay in the Hametoon overnight. We walked over the hill to Cole. Coats were thrown on a bed upstairs, and outdoor boots left there too. Downstairs the table was moved to the side of the room and there were bench seats. People from East Burrafirth, Gonfirth, Voe and Muckle Roe were there. The area for dancing was very small and we had to keep off the open fire. Tea was made ben – I don't think the cups were ever washed. There was no bread board so Jannie, whose house it was, sliced the loaf against her breast.

When I was old enough to go to Cole dances with Auntie Ellen's approval, we walked first to Skeetalea, where John joined us with his fiddle. Next stop was the Ladie, then Houbanster, where John played the fiddle and we danced in each house before those inhabitants joined us on the walk to Cole.

52

Da Nort Store

Da NORT STORE at Gudataing (which stood nearest the head of the pier) was built in 1902 and the other, built on to the back, was erected in the early 1930s. There was no road down to the shop until about 1925. It got the name of da New Rodd and as far as my generation is concerned it still gets that name today (which is a bit ironic considering we still didn't have our new road at Burrafirth until about 10 years later). The road proved a great boon to the shop as lighter goods could be transported by a lorry which was owned by Andy Moffat at Gerts.

As far as I can remember the North of Scotland steamer still came once a fortnight until shortly before the Second World War. When the first store was built there was a small area partitioned off in which Tammie Anderson kept a cow; so that area was referred to as the byre, even after the partition was removed and that area of space provided extra storage for heavy goods, which came by sea.

Da Nort Store was also a fine big area for social functions. There were a few wedding receptions held there before the hall was ready for functions – Andrew Clark and Christina Robertson (married at Aith Church in September 1921); Ruby Tait and Walter Jamieson (December 1921); Mary Jane Tait and Tammie Williamson (December 1922); Jessie Moffat and Andrew Robertson (March 1926) and Mootie Hunter and Robbie Leask (April 1926). There may have been others, but during the 1920s a lot of marriages took place at Lerwick. Some had their reception in Lerwick, while others held a hamefare in the home of the bride's parents.

Anyway, I have been told that a notice was put up in the shop asking all the young men to come along at a given time to clear the store. I suspect functions would have been timed for the week before the steamer was expected when stores would have been low. I have no doubt there would have been no shortage of volunteers to lift all the remaining goods and stack them up securely into a pile in the byre. It may all have been covered over by a tarpaulin; the floor swept clean and benches arranged to accommodate those young folk who were ever eager to attend. They came to those homely functions from Clousta and from Twatt; and young men from much further afield would come on bicycles to partake of lively entertainment.

53

Box Socials at Aith

AMONG the most popular entertainment in da Nort Store were box-socials and dances. I do not know for certain how often these were held, but somehow I think it could have been once a month, perhaps from October to March. Box-socials were also held in Twatt school – maybe on alternate weeks from those held in da Nort Store. But that is only a guess of my own, and may not be correct. Box-socials were held all over Shetland at this period, as it was a popular way of raising money for whatever project was in mind; they raised a lot of money towards the cost of a hall. At Aith, box-socials were often held in the public hall long after it got erected.

I feel there might be a need to explain to younger readers what a box-social actually was. Mind you, they were in their heyday before I was old enough to prepare a box or to have a boyfriend! But I have memories of Liza baking bannocks, queen cakes etc. in readiness for filling her box.

What I remember most was that small tin of Fray Bentos corned beef which she opened very carefully, then forked the contents into a bowl, added a small amount of water to sort of make it moist, then a dash of HP sauce to add a taste. She had the flour bannocks split open with a light spread of butter or margarine before filling in the bully-beef to make a tasty sandwich. John Robert and I would be kneeling on chairs with elbows on the table waiting hopefully for a chance that she might leave some of that mixture for us to lick out with a spoon. In our house, bully-beef was indeed a rarity. It would have taken a few large tins to have made a meal for a large family. Gingerbread and other goodies also went into the box as well as a packet of 10 cigarettes.

I also need to explain how the basic box was procured in the first place. In those days, bars of chocolate from Fry's or Cadbury's came in hard cardboard boxes about 8 inches by 12 inches and four inches deep. After the chocolate had been sold at Aith shop those boxes were kept and handed over to those looking for something suitable to use as a social box. Usually the cardboard lid was still attached.

First of all, the box was usually covered with material of some sort. There were always those who had artistic ideas how to make their handiwork look nice and original. I will try to describe one such box which Mimie Ellen at Bonhouse had once bought at a box social. In it she kept a pile of old photographs, which I so often turned over during those days of my childhood. It was covered in royal blue velvet with padding underneath so as to give the lid a slightly raised appearance; right in the middle of the lid was a postcard picture of the Scott Monument in Princess Street, Edinburgh; a piece of postcard size glass covered the picture while silver tinsel had been stitched along the border of the picture. It was a bonny box.

I regret very much that I didn't think to ask Matthew for that box after Mimie Ellen's death. It still holds good memories for me. It would be interesting to discover whether any of those decorated boxes still survive from those years of long ago.

It was usually the young, unmarried girls who prepared those social boxes, though I have been told that there were odd occasions when the men had a chance. Money was scarce, especially after the First World War. Young men, home from the Merchant Navy, went on the dole but that benefit didn't amount to much. Knitting brought in a little for the girls and women, but everyone had to be very careful how money was spent.

There would have been maybe a bit of competition as to who could produce the prettiest box; there seemed also to have been an element of excitement and secrecy with a box social. "Wha tinks du will buy dy box or my een?" Who can say how some of those young hearts would have gone pit-a-pat when hers (or his) was held up for auction – or whether, by the end of the evening, there could have been a sense of disappointment and let-down? If a girl had a serious boyfriend he would have been let in on the secret of how her box had been decorated, so he would be able to identify his lady-love's creation when it came up for sale.

Those dainty boxes needed to be carefully wrapped in brown paper (or whatever) to protect them from the elements for, of course, there were no motorcars, and in the case of those girls from East Burrafirth a skyiff took them across the narrow voe, after which they still had quite a long walk around the east side of Aith Voe and down to the Nort Store at Gudataing. One can't help wondering how they managed for there was still no road down to the shop area and they had no such thing as Wellington boots.

To confuse their would-be lads, the girls were in the habit of swapping boxes, so young fellows needed to keep their wits about them – just in case a mistake was made, thereby letting their best girl down, which could easily have led to a 'fit o' da snippers'! Nae winder some of them were on tenterhooks.

At this stage let me tell you of an occasion which Liza related to me many years ago. They had been at a social when men had provided the boxes. Surely, to make sure that his lady love would have no difficulty in identifying his box, a certain fellow had a novel idea. He went along to the shop and purchased an enamel bucket. He maybe got his sister's help to get the necessary items for eats, besides chocolates for her and cigarettes for himself. Anyway, all those young folk walking back to East Burrafirth overtook this couple. There they were on the road at Scarvataing, he seated on the bucket with his girlfriend perched on his knee!

On reaching the Nort Store at Gudataing the boxes were either set out on a table or a bench. Then the auctioneer got going. Not everyone had the natural knack to do such a job but I have been told that Geordie Dalziel from Stiva took it upon himself to exhort a few extra shillings from would-be buyers. If Geordie Dalziel wasn't available then Andrew Mitchell from Twatt was asked to do the job.

Sometimes, the boxes weren't auctioned, but were drawn by numbered tickets. The boxes were priced at two shillings (10p) each which certainly wasn't much, but then two shillings was of value to anyone who didn't possess much money. Those who brought a box wrote their names on a bit of paper and stuck it on the inside of the lid. I'm not certain where tea would have been made – maybe in the house of Gudataing. So when the time came for that refreshment then each couple – the maker and the buyer – sat together and partook of the contents of the box.

On one occasion Duncan Leask from Sandsound bought three tickets at two shillings each. He would have had the pick of the draw, after which he handed the other two boxes to a couple of young fellows who perhaps found it hard to buy a ticket. I daresay they wouldn't have minded whose box came their way. Hungry boys would have been more interested in all the eatables within.

Apparently the evening was rounded off by a good going dance with all those auld fashioned dances – eightsome reels, lancers, quadrilles, Boston and more than likely a Scotch reel and a Shetland reel; maybe the Haymakers and the Foula reel and more of the older dances. Certainly there would not have been line dancing. They knew all about lines – 'dellin a rig wi twa geng o' spades'! Tammie Abernethy from Tresta played music on his fiddle. Maybe others who could play did a turn and more than likely someone played a concertina or maybe a trump (Jew's Harp).

Circa 1927/28: these are some of the folk who went to the box socials. Left to right: Johnnie Anderson (Voehead) and his sisters Ruby and Katie with their first cousins from Slyde, Liza and Tom.

54

Aith Hall

THE man who got the contract to build Aith Hall was from Unifirth; his name was Christopher Irvine. I do not have the names of those other workmen who were employed on that job. I have been told that some men worked for free; but I am not certain whether that is true or not. Certainly wages at that time would have been very, very low and local employment non-existent.

Some men were employed in the transportation of shingle by flit boats from the spit of sand at the Ayres! Stones, too, came from the points of Scarvataing and Hestataing for the foundation. All that building material had to be unloaded at the pier at Gudataing then transferred into a small cart which was then pulled by a pony up to the building site. Finer sand for plastering got flit from Da Geo o' Keeng which is situated on the back of Aithsness.

All that hard manual labour is a far cry from modern machinery used in today's building projects. Christie Irvine and his band of labourers had every right to be proud of Aith Hall by the time it was complete and ready for the opening ceremony which took place on 24th November, 1927. I have not discovered whether someone made a speech to mark the occasion or not. A sale-of-work was held on that date which was well supported, and which turned in some much needed money. The original cost of that hall was in the region of £800, a big sum of money in the 1920s. I shouldn't think there would have been any grants in those days.

I wasn't present at the hall opening. At the time I would have been aged ten. More than likely all the children of my age (and younger) who lived near the head of the voe would have been there, but in the backwoods of East Burrafirth bairns were sort of kept on a backburner until they reached school leaving age at fourteen! I can well remember my oldest brothers cutting up the carcass of a fat hog and stowing it into a cardboard box all in readiness to be transported to that sale. The women folk did some knitting too – but muggins just looked on.

Getting water

When Aith Hall first got underway there was no running water, no mod cons of any sort. There was a door on the back wall of the kitchen through which water from a well below the manse had to be transported in buckets. Young lads, of an age when they maybe felt too embarrassed to ask their favourite girls on to the dance floor, seemed always more willing to be water-carriers. Who can say, they might have noticed more of the game than those who sat upon the seats along the sides of the hall!

Anyway, during the process of a wedding, after hours of dancing attendance on the guests and dancing all those heavy dances on the floor, there, of course, came a need to commune with nature. A group of three or four girls would team up to run the gauntlet through a group of men who forever seemed to be milling around in the outer porch at the north end of the hall, opposite the door of the ladies cloakroom. Often, some of them bore the signs of having had a few swigs from a bottle of Johnnie Walker. On thinking back, I feel sure we felt there was safety in numbers; especially on a dark evening, when there was no option but to go free range! Of course, there could have been those who got ambushed on the inward journey. There may have been a few who wished to be waylaid, but I can only speak for myself, who always made a wild dash back into the cloakroom to have a tidy-up before re-entering the main hall.

This brings to mind being at a function in the Brae Hall where a curtain across a corner of the ladies' cloakroom screened an enamel bucket. When the bucket was nearly full a couple of hefty women drew back the curtain, opened the window and emptied the bucket – presumably anyone lurking outside would have moved quickly as soon as they became aware of the window opening!

Soon after the mains water reached this district there was some sort of lean-to built on the north end of the hall and flush toilets came into being, which was a great improvement. I wonder what the youth of today would think if they had need to endure the privations of long ago. As I think I've written earlier, they don't know they are alive! I will admit though, that they have things to worry about which never entered our simple existence all those years ago.

Weddings in Aith Hall

The very first wedding held in Aith Hall took place in January 1929, when Ina Moffat, Gerts, and Duncan Leask from Sandsound married. In February 1930, Mimie Ann Johnson, Ayres, and Robbie Anderson, Lochside, held their reception; and from then on many a wedding took place. I have quite a collection of wedding invitation cards, and have discovered that from 1929 to 1950 there were almost forty weddings in Aith Hall. From October 1937 until January 1938 there were five weddings.

In those days whole families got invited to attend the church service and the reception, so often the hall was packed out. The bridal party and guests walked from the church to the hall, sometimes with a fiddler leading the way. On arrival at the hall I forget if tea and sandwiches were served (as happened in 1950s) or if they had to wait till suppertime. Much later, it became fashionable to invite nearest relations and close friends to church etc. with special invitation cards sent out to younger folk to attend the dance only.

A door near the south end of the hall (sheltered by a small porch) gave access to the kitchen and also to a stairway which led to an upstairs committee room. At those weddings of long ago tables were set up there for supper; I think there was room for sixty guests to be seated at once. The supper usually consisted of sliced roast and boiled mutton; tea and bread, with homebakes perhaps, too, and fancy biscuits. There may have been trifle. It was hard work running up and down those stairs carrying whatever was needed but there were plenty of helpers.

Supper started to be served soon after 9pm. An announcement was made from the platform; it was usually the older guests who went up first. Soon a queue began to form between the main hall and the foot of the stairs; everyone gazing upwards in anticipation of a tasty supper! It took a big strong man to hold them back while dirty dishes were carried down to the kitchen and tables re-laid for another sitting.

By midnight more hungry dancers joined the queue, and the alleyway between the main hall and the foot of the stairs was packed tight, with Muckle Ollie, whose loud voice was forever shouting, "Gangway please! Move back a bit." There was no space left for moving in any direction. One elderly gentleman once said that the crowd at the foot of the stairs on wedding nights reminded him of the pictures he had seen of starving children outside Dr Barnardo's!

Mind you, those weddings of long ago carried on until four or five in the morning. Some of those who had already had a supper around midnight were ready for another before dancing stopped. I don't remember food ever running short, nor a time set to end the serving of suppers.

Through time, a limit was set on how many guests got invited to a wedding, so that by about 1960, tables were set up in the main hall and a full meal served right at the beginning of the reception. That is the pattern which most weddings follow at the present time, so it's only we aulder folk who remember all the work which went into those suppers in the upper room! There was no shortage of helpers otherwise it would have been impossible to carry it all through.

Contrary to some younger folk's opinion, the Aith Hall was never a Rechabite Hall, but the committee of the day observed an unwritten law that alcoholic drink was not to be served. So only port and other wine and soft drinks were poured out for wedding toasts! Needless to say, those who wished to have a taste of a 'drap o' da hard' brought along their own bottles, which got passed around out of doors. I don't know for certain, but I have been told that not until a wedding in 1950 did the barman and bridegroom make a decision to take no notice of the so-called ban, and spirits were openly served to the wedding guests.

At those weddings of long ago there were no fancy greeting cards available, but those who couldn't attend a wedding usually sent greetings by telegram. Sometimes the message would be witty; I can only remember a few favourites:

"Lang may your lum reek."

"May more than a fence run round your garden."

"May all your spuds be golden wonders."

"Wi Willie for skipper and Willa as mate, the crew will sign on at a later date."

"Wi Tirval for skipper and Tamar as mate, there'll be room on the boat for a far bigger crew."

"May the knot that's been tied today never be a granny."

"May da couples abune never faa in, an da couple below never faa oot."

"May aa your troubles be peerie tings."

And another unusual one went something like this: "Turkey when you're hungry; champagne when you're dry; fifties when you're hard up and heaven when you die."

"One and one make two, they say, but if those two should marry, just you wait a year or two – there'll be two and one to carry!"

When my niece Jean married Alan Leask, someone sent the message: "Alan, du's taen a Slyde in da richt direction."

Dances

A new hall called for more modern dances. Gone were the days when a Shetland reel or a Scots reel were favourites, although they have been revived in recent years. The very first time that I remember being in Aith Hall I was taken by Uncle Christie and Mimie Ellen to a concert followed by a dance, to welcome the New Year of 1929.

I remember one couple who tried to dance a new American dance – the Charleston. It was a bit of a fiasco. The gentleman may have seen it danced somewhere but his partner certainly had not had such an opportunity. It was meant to be danced in very quick time with fancy side kicks. I imagine, too, Tammie Abernethy's fiddle may not have been equal to all the intoning of special notes needed for such a dance. In my mind's eye, I see them still trying out that new get-up, with the whole dance floor to themselves.

One-steps came into fashion, and two-steps. Most of us, I'm sure, never knew exactly the difference between them. I reckon my short legs weren't long enough for the long gliding steps of the latter. Square dances were the favourites, especially the lancers and quadrilles, besides a Boston and waltzes. Through time, we progressed to the Lambeth Walk and Bumps-a-Daisy, besides many others. One vivid memory remains when a fellow of short stature came in and asked a girl for a Boston. She was a really tall girl and heftily built, too. He, who had too much drink on board, never let go of her hand and had no idea of the dance steps. It was an amusing sight, reminding me of somebody taking a young calf for his first trip outside on the end of a short rope. Of such are the memories of youth.

The onlookers

When I was a teenager, I somehow became aware, in a sub-conscious way, of those dark, sparkling, all-seeing eyes of that row of elderly women who made sure of a vantage seat, usually on a bench along the wall near the door. They sat in a tight row, making sure nothing passed their attention – forever nudging each other and whispering their secret of what they had noticed on the dance floor: who danced most often with whom; whose husband got too much drink, etc. Human nature never changes; it's just times that change. There's nothing new under the sun, or the moon, for that matter. The onlooker always sees most of the game!

I daresay it would have been a source of entertainment for them and could easily have given some of them a clue as to which way the wind blew! Some of the clever ones, who may indeed have had a gift of second sight, would have put two and two together and got six for an answer!

Anyway, as the years passed, it became clear that it was time for my generation to take a back seat, and so we became the onlookers of the game. Youth, with its boundless energy, passes by all too quickly, though it is only with hindsight that this truth becomes apparent, as time keeps speeding onwards.

The main difference between then and now is that, at any hall function nowadays, the amplified music from the band forces folk to shout to neighbours to get the message across. Soon the effort becomes too much, so conversation stops. But there will always be those who are eager to discover what the future might hold for those young folk; though for my own part I feel content to wait and see what happens ... time aye tells!

Dressing for a wedding

Long dance dresses came into fashion in the 1930s though, if I remember right, those were worn only at weddings in our neck of the woods. It was not an easy journey from our home at Slyde to get to a wedding in Aith Hall, but I don't remember the weatherman ever stopping us. The long dresses had to be taken in a bag of some sort, along with dance shoes. Sometimes the change of dress took place at the Voehead in Aith, where my cousins lived. Even so, there was still a bit to walk to witness a marriage in the kirk. For the life of me I can't recall how we managed. Maybe sometimes the change-over took place in the hall cloakroom.

I can remember once or twice some of us girls going to Navy Cottage before the dancing began, so as to have the skirts of our dresses ironed. This was done by standing near the kitchen table, spreading out the flared skirt of the dress while Annie Tait stood ready with the smoothing iron in an effort to 'tak oot da lirks'. I have very few memories of the homeward journeys before a road came to our toonship; we, no doubt, bucksed through dubb and mire – always glad to get home and into a warm bed.

August 1940: Jeemie Sandison.   *1940: the author.*

Going to a wedding, early 1940s

I have one vivid memory of going to a wedding. This time three of us females decided we would cross the voe in a small skyiff, from the Wasthoose noost across to the East Noost at Hestataing. We were wearing hats! And rubber boots! My niece Jean and I had an oar each, while the other passenger, whose name I won't mention, sat on the aftertaft.

Just as we reached the middle of the mouth of the voe and came into the wind (which was blowing from the west), one of those squally showers set up and began to patter us with raindrops. I was on the weather side and tried to hold my head into the wind in an effort not to lose my hat. Our passenger got frightened and began to shout, "I'm goin ta jump! I'm goin ta jump!" What could I have done to stop her anyway? I remember saying, "Du'll jüst hae ta jimp if du feels laek it, dere's as much water as will cover dee!" Anyway, she sat still, clutching the gunnels of the skyiff in a vice-like grip.

On reaching the other side safely (if slightly drookled), we had need of those rubber boots, for we had to make sure we pulled the skyiff right above high tide mark and make it fast. What a hassle that was. More than likely we left those rubber boots at Hestataing. Thankfully by that time long dresses were not what we wore to a wedding.

When my generation was young, it was usual that once a couple got married they gave up going to dances, though of course attended weddings, where those couples who had the notion to dance still did so. Of course, there are those with no sense of rhythm who don't really enjoy dancing. Then there was another reason, which a young married mother referred to: "Tak da flounces fae dy goon; mak a goonie tae dy loon; for dy dancin days ar dön, bonnie lassie o!"

Hall improvements

In the early 1980s, the original hall got completely renovated. The stairs which led to the room above got demolished and the whole building took on a new look, though I am pleased we can still admire Christie Irvine's handiwork in the beautiful ceiling of the big hall. I have been told that the full cost was in the region of £81,000, compared with £800 for the very first building. The opening of this building took the form of a dinner and dance on 16th April, 1982. Since then the hall has been extended and improved at least twice, and all visitors are impressed with the very high standard of facilities.

Section 9

Marriage

55

Early Married Life

Marriage

In 1932, a Sandison family from Northmavine moved to Hestataing, and apparently it was my destiny to marry one of the sons, Jeemie, who was one year older than me. Ours was a wartime marriage. There was no time and less money to prepare for a hall wedding. Jeemie, who had been in the Merchant Navy before the war, joined the Naval Rescue Tugs in early 1942. We made plans to get married on his first leave in August. Faider was very hard of hearing by this time so I waited till I had the privacy of just us two off fishing in the voe before telling him of my wedding plans.

As soon as I got word that Jeemie was on his way home, I cycled off to get our marriage banns. Jeemie arrived home on a Saturday and we set off to Lerwick on the Monday. There I bought a dress, coat, hat and shoes and even an iced cake from Malcolmson's Bakery. My dress was mid blue (thank heavens those days of wearing black were long past) with a plain skirt, a lace bodice and short lace sleeves. The coat was woollen material in light blue with dashes of other colours – navy and orange, I think. Shoes and hat were navy. On Wednesday, 19th August, 1942, Edmund Tait was hired to take us to the Manse of Sand, Sandsting, where we were joined in marriage by the Rev. Norman Robinson. Returning to Slyde we had a sit down meal with family and a few close friends.

Next forenoon – and every other forenoon for a week – Jeemie took his motor cycle and rode to Lerwick in order to report to headquarters – such was the law and restrictions during World War Two.

August 1940: Jeemie Sandison and the author. Like all other bridal couples at that time, the bridal party made a special trip to the photographer's studio in Lerwick a day or two after the marriage.

1942: Jeemie and the author with Jeemie's sister, Annie, and the author's nephew, George.

Our first home

We started married life at Slyde but I was encouraged to look for a house for ourselves. *The Shetland Times* was delivered by the postman who often stopped and enjoyed a cup of tea at Slyde. In the time he did this, I scanned the newspaper and wrote a letter in response to an advert I saw for a property to rent in Weisdale. To keep the family in the dark, I caught the postman as he reached the gate at the top of our road as he left and gave him the letter to post. In due course, I cycled with Annie, Jeemie's sister, to view the house and agreed to rent it.

Having been to the saleroom in Lerwick to buy a chest of drawers, dresser, bed, table and couch, we moved into a peerie, wood-lined, wood-floored, thatched-roofed house, known as South Houll, in Weisdale, on 15th July, 1943. I took a kyist from Slyde and a small square of lino. We stained the wooden floor and laid the lino in the centre. One aunt gave us a stove; another gave lino for the ben-end. Peats for the ben fire were flit from East Burrafirth and built in a stack at the road. In the stove we used coal. I was given my grandmother's tattit rug which I cut up to make three small rugs.

Though I had known very few folk at Weisdale, I soon felt at home; the neighbours were extremely friendly and kindly. I had a happy three years there, doing my own thing. All that time Jeemie was at home for only short leave. Apart from curing peat, away up on the hill in sight of Sandwater, I had no crofting responsibilities, though I often helped neighbours with their work.

Our first child, Jeemsie, was born in that house in Weisdale in 1944. Jeemie asked for leave till the baby was born; he didn't have to tell me this had been refused for I remember him coming home with a face like thunder. He was in Portsmouth when he got the telegram to tell him about the baby – he was allowed some home leave then.

Move back to East Burrafirth

In July 1946, Jeemie got demobbed. He felt we had need to go back to Hestataing as by this time his parents were both over 70; the croft still had to be cultivated and peats to be cured. Tradition was that a son helped the older people and my family impressed upon me that it was my duty to move to Hestataing. The Swedish houses at Weisdale were still only pie in the sky, as were the first council houses in Aith, so there was really no alternative but to live with my parents-in-law, and Annie, my sister-in-law. However, we managed to pull together not too badly.

Employment was hard to come by after the war ended so, in 1948, Jeemie joined those whalers who went to South Georgia. Many weeks sometimes would pass before we got a letter, but many others were in the same position.

Getting a mains water supply and also electricity made quite a big difference to our life-style – no more carrying buckets of water from the well (or the burn for washing in). No more smelly lamps to fill with paraffin.

By this time the smallest shops were closed but we were well served by travelling shop vans from the Aith and Bixter shops, as well as the big green Co-op van from Lerwick, the butcher van from Weisdale and at least one fish van each week. However, I remember one occasion, about 1955, after a snow storm, the van from the Bixter shop got stuck in a drift somewhere along the road and was unable to deliver our five-gallon drum of paraffin. Strong wind prevented us going by sea to Aith shop. At that time Jeemie's fourteen-year-old nephew, Billy Nicolson, was attending Aith Secondary School and lodged with us at Hestataing as there was no daily school transport from Tresta to Aith. Billy and I set off for Gudataing with another empty five-gallon drum to get paraffin for light. Anyway, it ended up with each of us carrying a bag of messages on our back and that drum with four gallons of paraffin between us! We encountered snowdrifts in places, and I remember singing to Billy, "I will never ever complain when the rain licks down. Never again will I lay oot at rain." What a struggle that was!

56

Remembering the Big Snow, 1947

FINALLY, an attempt to give some details of what conditions were like in the spring of 1947, still referred back to by those of us who are old enough to remember.

Many years have passed since that 'lang-lying snaa' which covered most of Britain, and although there have been many blizzards since, none lay so long. Even the blizzard which came at Christmas 1995 – though it built up huge snowdrifts (said to be up to 30 feet in places), the like of which the younger generation had never experienced before – never got a really hard crust on top, and after 10 or 12 days it had all disappeared.

The snow which came in the spring of 1947 caused roads to be blocked for six weeks. Much to my regret, I hadn't thought to be keeping a diary all those years ago, so am having to rely on my memory and some memories of others too. There could well be some of you out there who did keep a day-to-day record of events, especially those who tried to keep things ticking over.

As usually seemed to happen in those days, it began to snow a little, on and off, towards the end of January, which left only a very slight covering. But on 22nd February it came on a blizzard, good and proper, from an easterly direction. I remember that Andy Moffat at the Gerts died on March 12th. His funeral was on the 14th. Roads, that day, were pretty hazardous, but by the next day they were blocked by snow.

The snow clearing equipment of those days was inadequate to deal with such a situation. So, after a few futile attempts, the council concentrated their efforts in keeping the road open between Lerwick and Scalloway, so as to give some access to and from the West Side. Otherwise, all transport was by sea.

Once the clouds had emptied out their loads of snow, the sun shone out and the wind remained fairly light. Jack Frost took over with low temperatures, so that the whole snow field took on a hard crust which sparkled in the sunshine.

It stayed that way until well towards the end of March by which time, owing to longer hours of daylight, the thick snow blanket slowly gave over to the strong rays of sunshine. This was referred to as a 'dry tow', as opposed to an 'up-lowsin' which means a quick thaw that tends to leave much destruction in its wake.

Of course, there was no electricity or a piped water supply all those years ago, so that meant fetching water from the well to water cows, as well as for household occupants. I daresay we melted snow to help out. There was a good supply of peats near at hand so fires were kept going, but it would have been pretty hard on old folk with no young ones to help. But in those days there seemed to be very few people living on their own and, if there were, then kindly neighbours would have seen to their needs, or maybe even taken them into their own family home so as to be sure of their safety.

At that time I was into the eighth month of pregnancy so I wasn't fit to do much outside at all. I remember trying to fetch water from the well, which lay quite a bit from our house, and across a burn, with a narrow plank bridge, but owing to the depth of snow on each side of a shovelled-out pathway I had to admit defeat. So it became one of Jeemie's morning chores to make two or three trips to the well with buckets for water – enough to fill up every available container. The well was always kept well covered and had a marker so that it was easy to find after fresh snowfalls.

Jeemie's parents, and sister Annie, attended to the feeding and other needs of the cows in the byre and lambs in lambhouse. It was a major operation. Neeps and kale had to be thawed out; I remember neeps sometimes put under the restin chair, and a kishie of kale hearts standing in the porch, to make them frost free. Another of Jeemie's sisters, Mary, who was married and lived in Unst, had come down for a week or two before the snow laid on. So she and her two peerie boys got snow-bound and never got home again until the beginning of April.

Being cooped up in our house together, too young to be outside in the deep snow, our son Jeemsie, aged 2½ years, and his cousin Richard, who still hadn't reached his second birthday, got fairly browned off with each other.

Toys were few and space was limited, so eventually they took to biting each other whenever they found themselves in a corner! An eagle eye needed to be kept on them but there was little new with which to distract them.

So it was that there were six adults and three young children all together under our roof at Hestataing, which at that time was only three rooms with low attic rooms above, and no bathroom. We had none of the facilities which young people of today regard as a necessity; they don't know they're alive, nor any of those hardships endured by a former generation.

When I decided to attempt to write my memories about the 1947 snow, I had to rake through my memory box and that of others, in an effort to discover most of the details. Everyone, of course, has their own memories and many a story could be told.

Sea Routes Revived

Having described the domestic scene I'll now write something of how transport by sea took place in this district that spring. Earlier, in the autumn of 1946, Malcolm Nicolson, Ollie Tait and Jeemie Sandison procured a small 28ft keel fishing boat, named *Myra*; a fine handy peerie boat which they used to set up a lobster fishing venture. It didn't prove to be a money-making project, but in those early post-war years times were poor and there was still little or no local employment. With the onset of that heavy snow it became more or less an impossibility to ship live lobsters to Billingsgate market in London.

However, owing to that big freeze up, they were called upon to transport goods ashore from the *Earl of Zetland*, which besides her usual runs to the North Isles etc., made at least two runs during the 1947 snow around the West Side, with essential food supplies for Walls, Aith, Brae and Hillswick. Then the need arose for the transport of bread from Adie's bakeshop at Voe. The *Myra* and her crew did quite a number of runs from Voe to Hillswick, Sandness, and here to our shop at Gudataing. I assume Brae shop would have had its own transport. In Clousta supplies got landed at the pier alongside the school then were carried by the waiting men across to the shop at da Grind.

In between those bread delivery runs, the boatmen baited long lines. At ebb tide mussels were gathered, or should I say, prised off daek-ends and piers. The daek-end between Hestataing and Selkieburn produced an abundance of mussels. Lines were taken down and hooks were baited. There was any amount of fish to be caught (how times have changed!), the lines being laid in Swaarbacks Minn – between the Muckle Roe lighthouse and Northra Voe (on the Isle of Vementry).

We got supplied with an abundance of fresh fish, mostly cod, one of which weighed 40lbs (18kg). Jeemie put a rope through its gills and dragged it up over the snow to the house. So we feasted on raans, crappen, and fried cod and cod 'taen da saut' – good food, which maybe a generation of today might not relish, used as they are to all the so-called fast foods. Back in 1947, everybody prepared for snow the previous autumn, by having a half barrel of salt herring and reestit mutton, besides a crö of tatties in the barn. Most folk, especially in the crofting community, were usually well prepared.

Hills all over Shetland took on a heavy load of snow. Sheep were found dead in layers under those deep drifts. Even if any got out alive there was nothing to feed them on. Some who had access to the ebb filled themselves with waar and tang but that in itself wasn't enough. Some crofters lost every sheep they had. I don't know whether there would have been any help from our government to restock. I very much doubt it. Those young sheep in the lambhouse fared better, but I expect their daily intake of fodder would have been rationed.

But those frozen-in conditions were hardest on those who were ill and needed hospital treatment. On at least two occasions Aith lifeboat was called upon to transfer patients to Scalloway where an ambulance would be ready to take the patient to Lerwick.

Our district nurse, who had been here for a few years, left in January and a replacement was due to arrive. She came on the North Boat to Lerwick, then to Scalloway and from there by sea to Reawick, where I have no doubt she had patients to attend to. It so happened that two babies were due in Aith in late March, mine at Hestataing and one at the Gerts.

Nurse Chris Robson had to be transported again by sea from Reawick to Bixter and from there she travelled on a sledge pulled by a Shetland pony owned by Cathy Georgeson. Laurie Tait from the Gerts was there too, armed with a shovel with which to smooth out a pathway for the sledge. Nurse Robson got accommodation beside the Laurensons at Sunnybank. I expect she would have made her visits to Adalina Tait at the Gerts by walking along the ebb, as that was quite a short cut between Gudataing and those croft houses on the west side of Aith Voe. But that was impossible on the east side, where the foreshore is much more strewn with rocks.

My niece, Jeannie Tait, at the Hametoon (who now lives at Bonhouse in Clousta), at that time was still under three years of age and had developed a nasty abscess on her limb. Her dad, Lollie Tait, got Alec Leask from the Hoit to come and get the nurse along to see Jeannie. That was in mid-March. I remember that was the first time she came to visit me. "I'm really worried about Mrs Tait's little girl, she should be in hospital," she said. Anyway, Alec and Lollie took Nurse Robson back to Aith where she managed to telephone Dr Budge at Parkhall. Dr Budge telephoned Dr Porter at Voe who suggested that someone come to Voe to collect M & B Tablets – those were the days before penicillin. So Alec and Lollie returned to Burrafirth, I daresay to let folk know what was next on the agenda!

When Jeemie returned on the *Myra* from that day's mercy trips and was ready to pick up the moorings, there was Lollie in his skyiff waiting to go on this trip to Voe. It was about 8pm, so away they went in bright moonlight, returning back nigh on midnight. Olnafirth, a dangerous place for ice most winters, never froze over that spring of 1947, owing to there being no fresh water from the two burns, which had been held back in Jack Frost's grip for many weeks. If it had frozen over it would have been very dangerous to go there with a wooden boat as the ice could have cut through the hull – this could have hampered not only this trip but the bread trips also.

For the next week or two Alec Leask took his motor boat to convey the nurse from Gudataing to the Hametoon every forenoon, except for once or twice on a Sunday when Jeemie Sandison did the trip with the *Myra*. Jeannie has a vague memory of that time she spent in a large crib and how terrified she was of the nurse and how she felt upset whenever anyone else who was a stranger happened along. That memory lay in with Jeannie for many months, but she slowly recovered. If penicillin had been available the cure would have been much quicker.

Adalina Tait, at the Gerts, gave birth to her daughter Christine in the last week of March, by which time most roads were passable for cars. I do not remember being worried or concerned about the impending birth of our second child, though I recall one darksome evening keeping a lookout in the nort end skylight for a sighting of the *Myra* returning from her Sandness trip, being a bit apprehensive at the thought of what we could do if my infant decided it was time to be born. My mother-in-law was reassuring, saying we would call on our neighbour, Betty Nicolson, at Scarvataing, so all would be well. Jeemsie was staying at Slyde until after the baby arrived.

It so happened that my baby stayed where she was, safe and snug, until All Fools Day was past! By then things were moving on all the roads again. My niece Jean Anderson from Slyde happened to come along on her pushbike just after teatime on 2nd April; she was sent post-haste to tell Nurse Robson to come. I remember Jean saying that she pedalled so fast that by the time she reached Sunnybank she was quite out of breath. Luckily Nurse had not long returned from being out somewhere but got into her car and raced to Hestataing.

Everything was over before 9pm and there was Thelma, safe and sound. Dr Budge had to come as I needed a stitch – I forget if there was a local anaesthetic first. Following the birth my temperature rose – milk fever I think – so I was glad of Nurse Robson's care over the following days. It was normal then to stay in bed for seven to ten days following childbirth. The maternity Annexe at Lerwick still hadn't been opened in April 1947. I may be wrong, but I think that event took place later that same year – October or November. What a godsend that proved to be to many a young mother and maybe for those not so young, besides the burden lifted from those at home. Maybe older children in a family would not have been too happy at Mam going away and coming back with another new baby. But that's how it still is.

That snow of 1947 still left its reminders by way of long stripes of white among higher hills well into the end of May. To compensate, or so we seemed to think, we had a splendid summer that year. Weeks of unbroken sunshine. Wells dried up – or at least some did – so that some folk had to flit water in wooden barrels. Little wonder how very thankful we were when a piped water supply could be turned on in the late summer of 1955.

Everything seems so different, and most of it I never try to keep up with nowadays; yet I can't help remembering. There was no such thing as bank loans or the never-never system. We were told never to buy anything unless we had the money with which to pay for it. Just to do without until you could afford whatever you had a mind on – and that was never very much.

For myself, I can only say that I feel glad to have lived to see so many improvements, and to see a younger generation enjoying the modern houses with all the mod-cons which we never had in our youth. Something has been lost along the way, but perhaps I feel like that since we gave up the crofting way of life and 'set wis at' in a sheltered house?

Life is still good; I have more time for other interests. I feel free from a lot of responsibilities and with more time to swing da lead. Pen and paper is good company, and I have much to be thankful for.

Soon the old ways will be entirely lost, if nothing gets written down.

It's good to remember the way it was and we auld codgers are happy with the way things are now. My generation has seen many changes and I don't think any of us would want a return to what's referred to as 'the good old days'. The only good thing was that we were young then, and youth can overcome all obstacles. Youth keeps looking ahead. But now, as I look back, I find it's good to recall the way it was.

Conclusion

57

Writing

I ALWAYS had an interest in poetry and I have composed quite a few poems and had them published in *Shetland Life* magazine. At Christmas 1985, I had a tape of poems – "Burrafirth Bruck" – released! To my surprise most of the tape was recorded, from memory, on the day I went to enquire about whether such a thing was possible. To be quite honest, I never felt chuffed over that project. Some day I may – or may not – get going to have my poems printed in a special edition of their own. That remains to be seen!

No matter what I try to write, I feel there's no way I could ever put across the way things once were. I feel sure my peerie stories may only be of interest to my own generation, as usually, when I meet with another who was young when I was young, then it's all the old days we recall. We don't seem to mind that we are unable to keep up with modern technology, although from watching television it's very rewarding to see how advanced science has become – which the youth of today tend to take for granted. I don't think they are any happier than we were when life was so much simpler and when most folk were contented with their lot.

Contentment means happiness, no matter what circumstances one might be in, but it is a state of mind which not everyone seems to possess.

How true is this poem I copied from an old *Shetland Almanac:*

Old Age

Age is the heaviest burden man can bear;
Compound of disappointment, pain and care.
For when mind's experience comes at length;

It comes to mourn the body's loss of strength.
Resigned to ignorance, all our better days.
Knowledge seems to ripen, as a man decays!
One ray of light – the closing eye receives
For wisdom only takes what folly leaves.

58

Philosophy

ALTHOUGH I have been ill many a time, I will admit that I recuperated quite quickly from whatever laid me low, so I daresay I have been lucky. I have been lucky, too, in having been gifted my father's placid nature. I don't get hett up over those petty things which overtake each and every one of us. When the hard blows come, my faith keeps me at peace. Ever since I left school I have been in the habit of writing down verses of poetry in notebooks – I make a point of sharing one of them with folk who are finding the going is hard. I keep records of all my correspondence so that recipients won't get the same verse twice.

The more one puts into life, the more one gets out of it, and I have proved this to be true over and over again. I get quite a few pleasant surprises, sometimes from a person I have never even met!

My hearing and eyesight have deteriorated considerably, my pace is slow now; the energy of youth and middle age is long gone; but when I needed to be strong I had a boundless amount of stamina. As far as I am aware, I still have all my marbles, and for that I never cease to be thankful. I have a good, caring family so I have been much blessed.

> Trust ye in Providence
> Providence is kind
> Bear ye all life's changes
> Wi a calm an tranquil mind
> Tho hemmed and pressed on every side
> Hae faith an you'll get through
> Every blade of grass has its ain drap o dew.

Appendices

HOUSEHOLD EVICTED FROM KERGORD, WEISDALE, IN 1869

These people moved to East Burrafirth, first to East Gate, then to Slyde

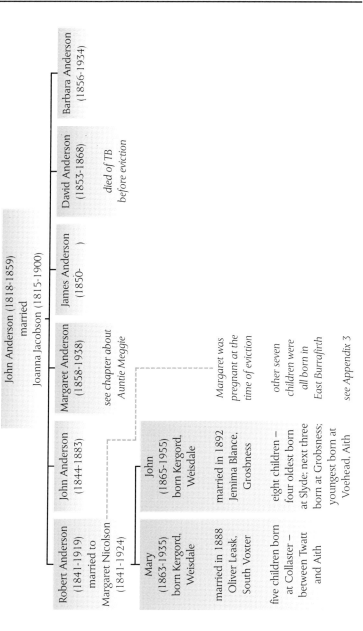

John Anderson (1818-1859)
married
Joanna Jacobson (1815-1900)

Barbara Anderson (1856-1934)

David Anderson (1853-1868)
died of TB before eviction

James Anderson (1850-   )

Margaret Anderson (1858-1938)
see chapter about Auntie Meggie

John Anderson (1844-1883)

John (1865-1955) born Kergord, Weisdale
married in 1892 Jemima Blance, Grobness
eight children – four oldest born at Slyde; next three born at Grobsness; youngest born at Voehead, Aith

Margaret was pregnant at the time of eviction

other seven children were all born in East Burrafirth

see Appendix 3

Robert Anderson (1841-1919) married to Margaret Nicolson (1841-1924)

Mary (1863-1935) born Kergord, Weisdale
married in 1888 Oliver Leask, South Voxter
five children born at Collaster – between Twatt and Aith

SECOND ANDERSON HOUSEHOLD EVICTED FROM KERGORD, BETWEEN 1871 AND 1879

The names of those who were evicted are **highlighted**

Robert Anderson (1789-1868) married **Robina** Duncan (1795-1879)

Children:

- John (1818-1859) married Joanna Jacobson (1815-1900)

  Joanna and her children were evicted in 1869 *see Appendix 1*

- Mary (1823-1917)

- Barbara (1827-1908)

- **James** (1829-1907) married **Janet** Laurenson

- David (1832-1861)

- Margaret (1835-1915)

- **Elizabeth** (1838-1923) this was the lady who chose Aithsness for her new home, causing two more families to be evicted

Children of **James** and **Janet**:

- Robert (1853-) later settled in Australia

- **Christina** (1855-1937) married in 1876 to William Nicolson, Mark, Aith — eleven children

- **James** (1858-1934) married in 1933 to Mary Smith — one daugher

- Elizabeth (1860-1948) married John Tait, Bonhouse, Clousta, lived at Greenmeadow, Clousta — nine children

- **Robina** (1863-1906) married in 1901 to Edmund Fraser, Edinburgh, see chapter 5 on 1904 boating accident — no family

- **Thomas** (1866-1920) unmarried, started first shop in Aith in 1900 had Gudataing house built

- **John** (1871-1904) unmarried see chapter 5 on 1904 boating accident

FAMILY OF PATERNAL GRANDPARENTS

John Anderson (1818-1859) married Joanna Jacobson (1815-1900)   Christopher Nicolson (1797-1880) married Marion Inkster (1806-1897)

Robert Anderson (1841-1919) married to Margaret Nicolson (1841-1924)

Mary (1863-1935)	John (1865-1955)	Thomas (1869-1963)	David (1872-1905)	Peter (1876-1903)	Robert (1880-1907)	James (1882-1924)	Christopher (1884-1952)	Joseph (1888-1976)
born Kergord, Weisdale married in 1888 to Oliver Leask South Voxter	born Kergord, Weisdale married in 1892 to Jemima Blance, Grobsness	born East Gate, East Burrafirth married Ann Jane Garrick	born Slyde, East Burrafirth married Willa Tait from Hametoon	born Slyde, East Burrafirth unmarried	born Slyde, East Burrafirth married in 1905 to Helen Garrick	born Slyde, East Burrafirth married in 1916 to Jessie Williamson Tumblin	born Slyde, East Burrafirth married in 1926 to Jemima Tait Bonhouse, Clousta	born Slyde, East Burrafirth married Lillie Renton, South Shields where they made their home
five children born at Collaster – between Twatt and Aith	eight children four oldest born at Slyde; next three born at Grobsness; youngest born at Voehead, Aith	see Appendix 5	died of TB at Cole, Gonfirth two months after youngest daughter died Widow and two other children eventually moved to Lochside, Aith	Lost at sea when the ship he was on foundered in Bay of Biscay when all hands were lost	see Appendix 5	lived at Sandsound killed in an accident on board ship while entering New York harbour in November 1924 no family	no family	three children, son Ronnie died aged 4 from rheumatic fever Joseph was on a ship which was in Hamburg at outbreak of WW1 so was POW throughout the war

FAMILY OF MATERNAL GRANDPARENTS

James Garrick (1847-1925) married to Elizabeth Tait (1849-1919)

Ann Jane (Jeannie) (1873-1919)	Cumming (1876-1895)	Barbara (1878-1927)	James John (1880-1882) *twins*	Laurence (1880-1916) *twins*	Helen (Ellen) (1881-1952)	James (1885-1941)	Robert (1887-1954)	Jemima (1892-1953)
married in 1895 to Tom Anderson from Slyde	unmarried	unmarried		unmarried	married in 1905 to Robbie Anderson from Slyde	married in 1912 to Margaret Sutherland, Sand	married in 1924 to Elizabeth Mouat	married in 1922 to John Mouat
spent married life at Slyde	died at sea near Falkland Islands when he lost his balance while making a sail fast, fell onto the deck and died four hours later; buried at sea the following day			seaman on HM Trawler *Kent* – died when a magazine exploded	lived at Slyde till her son, Peter, married; died at Tumblin	four sons Alec (1913-1973) John (1914-1989) Robbie (1917-1993) Willie (1918-1988)	four children Bobby (1924-) Agnes (1928-1979) Margaret (1930-) John (1933-)	three children Jeemie (1920-1962) Ella (1927-) Bessie (1929-)
see Appendix 5								these were the cousins I knew best on my mother's side of the family

SLYDE FAMILIES

Slyde would have been home address for most of the 1920s for the people whose names are **highlighted**. Seldom were they under the roof at one time as at least one of the men would have been away sailing. One winter I remember 11 of us at home together; that was probably after Robbie and Mimie's children were born.

Tom Anderson (Whistling Tom / Faider)
(1869-1963)

Tom's wife, Ann Jane (née Garrick) was Helen's older sister

Helen Anderson (née Garrick)
(1881-1952)

Widow of Robbie Anderson (Tom's brother) sister to Tom's wife

Tom
(1894-1929)
due to marry
Nanny Tait
from
Hametoon a
month after
his death

Robbie
(1896-1984)
married in
1920 to
Mimie Tait
from
Hametoon

two sons
one daughter
who were all
born and
brought up
at Slyde

Jeemie
(1900-1975)
married in
1923 to
Mary Tait
from
Braewick, Aith

two children
Tom
Wilma

John Robert
(1921-1985)

George
(1925-1999)

Jane (Jean)
(1928-1981)

Johnnie
(1902-1970)
married 1936
Mary Ann Tait
from
Upper Pund,
East Burrafirth

lived most of
married life at
Upper Pund,
East Burrafirth

three
daughters
Wilma
Margaret
Joyce

Eliza
(1905-1982)
married in
1932 to
Lollie Tait
from
Hametoon

lived at
Hametoon

see
Appendix 6

Davie
(1911-1929)
died on same
day as oldest
brother Tom

Maggie
(1913-2007)
spent most
of her life
at Slyde

Chrissie
(1917-   )
married in
1942 to
Jeemie
Sandison
from
Hestatating

lived most of
married life at
Hestatating
four children
Jeemsie
Thelma
Hazel
Alice

Peter
(1906-1978)
married in
1944 to
Babsy Tait
from
Hametoon

moved to
Tumblin after
married

no family

HAMETOON FAMILY

There were strong links between Slyde and the Hametoon family

Margaret (Maggie) (1889-1967)	Elizabeth (Betty) (1891-1931)	William (Willie) (1893-1902)	Jemima (Mimie) (1895-1977)	Anges (Nannie) (1899-1977)	Laurence (Lollie) (1902-1966)	Barbara (1902-1902)	Williamina (Mootie) (1905-1981)	Barbara (Babsy) (1907-1970)
married John Christie from Burra	married Willie Tait		married Robbie Anderson, Slyde	teacher at East Burrafirth	married Eliza Anderson, Slyde		married James Johnston	married Peter Anderson. Slyde double cousin to other Slyde spouses of her siblings
	Betty died a month after giving birth, leaving five young children			date had been set for marriage to Tom Anderson Slyde, for May 1929, the month after he died			lived at West Houlland – see chapter about learning to cycle	
no family	six children Frankie Barbara James (died 4 months) Maggie Laura Mary		three children John Robert George Jane (Jean)		six children Laurence Tammie Bobbie Bertie Jeannie Elma		three children Mitchell Betty Frank	no family

BONHOUSE FOLK

Andrew Tait (1830-1907) – he ran a shop at Bonhouse, Clousta

married (1) 1858 Lilias Manson (1836-1866)

married (2) 1887 Elizabeth Doull (1855-1947)

Children of the first marriage

Catherine (1859-1939)
married in 1883 John Jamieson from Setter, Clousta
emigrated to Australia
nine children all born in Australia

Jemima Helen (1860-1890)
married in 1887 Theodore Nicolson from Nesting
emigrated to USA
one daughter born in USA

John (1862-1903)
married in 1883 Elizabeth Anderson born in Kergord evicted from Kergord after 1871
see Appendix 2
when John's father married a second time, John and his family had to move out of Bonhouse where they'd lived after marriage

Mitchell (1865-1865)

Children of the second marriage

Andrew Matthew (1887-1969)
married in 1912 Margaret Bruce from Glasgow
Matthew spent most of his adult life in Glasgow; returned to Clousta after his wife died in 1952
two sons

Jemima Helen Brown (1891-1964)
married in 1926 Christopher Anderson from Slyde, East Burrafirth
no family

Frederick Bowie (1893-1958)
married (1) in 1925 Euphemia Moffat from Noonsbrough, Clousta
one son Freddy (1930-)
married (2) in 1948 Margaret Robertson from Grind, Clousta

The first two of their nine children were born in Clousta; the others were all born at Greenmeadow

THE SANDISON FAMILY WHO MOVED FROM ORBISTER (NORTHMAVINE) TO HESTATAING IN 1932

James Sandison (1874-1959) married to Ann (née Anderson) (1876-1961)

Joan (pronounced Joanne) (1909-2001)	Andrina (Annie) (1911-)	Mary (1914-2002)	James (Jeemie) (1916-1998)	John (Johnnie) (1919-1957)
married in 1940 to Willie Nicolson from Scarvataing	unmarried	married in 1944 to Danny Smith from Westing Unst	married in 1942 to Chrissie Anderson from Slyde	married in 1946 to Dorothy MacKay from Aberdeen
began married life at Burgans moved to Tresta when Cruden houses first built	lived at Hestataing for many years still lives in Aith	Mary met Danny while teaching in Unst the family later moved to Eshaness where Mary was teacher till she retired in 1974	began married life in Weisdale spent most of married life at Hestataing	spent married life in Aberdeen drowned when Fishery Cruiser *Vaila* ran aground
four children Billy Daisy Bert Ian		two sons Richard Donald	four children Jeemsie Thelma Hazel Alice	two sons Hamish Brian

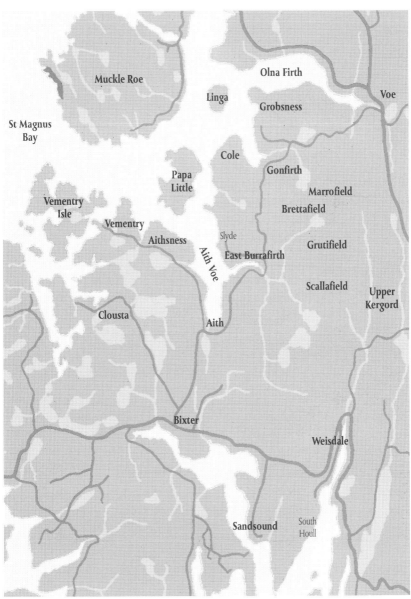

Map of author's boundaries.

257

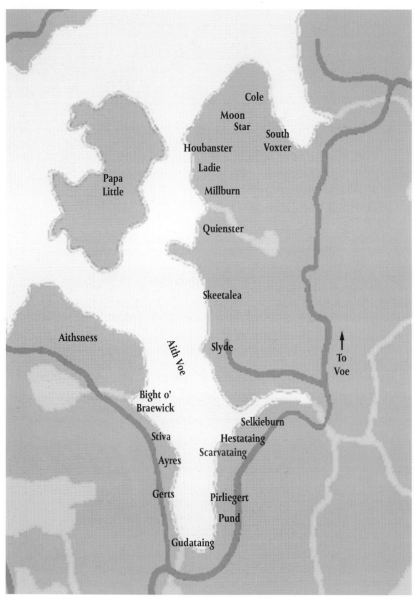

Map of Aith/East Burrafirth.

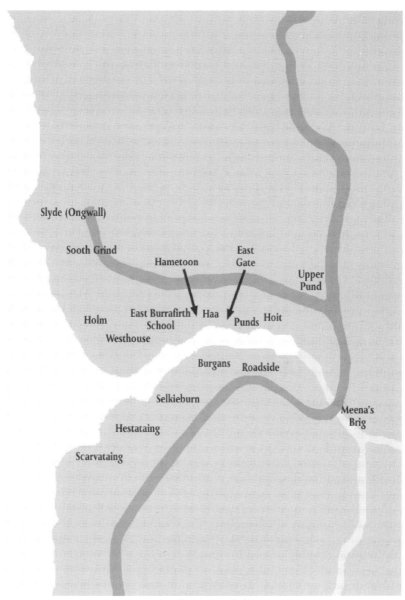

Map of East Burrafirth.

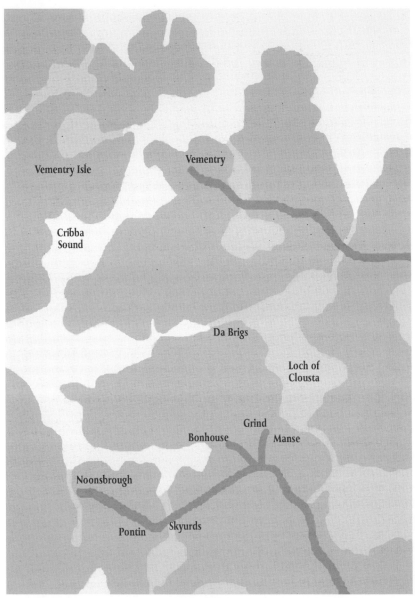

Map of Clousta.

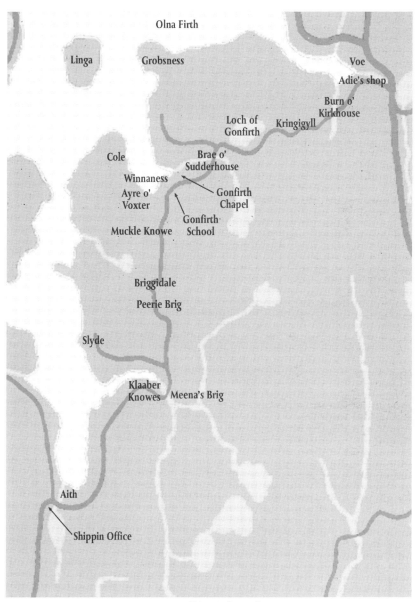

Map of Voe-Aith road.

Cat's Een i Da Dark

I winder if idder eens o you wis ever as scared as me
In dark an faersome places, wi nae idder body near?
Nae switches dan, tae licht da wye, or brichten up da gloom:
A faersome tocht hit truly wis, tae geng intae ony room.

A neuk apo da stairhead whar spinnin wheels an rowers wir keepit
Med a very cosy place indeed, as a böl fir Polly, da cat.
Nae faer sho laekely kettled dere, an sleepit oot mony a nap,
While aa da time, sho'd cock her lug fir a moose it wis shunned da trap.

Hit's a naitril thing fir bairns ta be kinda fairt i da dark,
Bit in my experience hit wis med waur be a lipper, low-doon hark.
In daylicht bricht I wis seen da cat lyin sleepin dere sae snug,
Ower young ta ken foo reflected licht med her een sae green an big.

Whin I wis peerie, da aulder eens med sure I wis weel telled
Aboot "green een itae da glory hol"; hit med you run pell mell;
Foo "he" sat dere an grinded his teeth, an glowered wi his muckle een,
An swished his tail, an sharpened his claas, ready ta mak a spring.

Gyaain upstairs wisna sae bad, fir dere wis licht below, and folk.
Bit comin doon! I could a sworn I felt his hot braith on me neck.
I wid grab fir da rail wi wan peerie haund – wi da idder een da rop –
An took wan headlang dive doon-trow; I could easy a brokken me back.

Me auldest sister, sho wis da wan dat startit aa dis faers.
Sae weel I mind dat winter's nicht, juist wis twa up da stairs.
A dyin fire wis aa da licht, da corners dey wir dark,
Sho bent doon, and in me lug, dis wirds sho began ta hark:

"Looks du, oot yonder, on da stairhead, whit's yon I tink I see,
Oot yonder i da glory hol? Looks du!" I lookit. Twa green een glowered at me!
I clutched her skirt, and held her fast, me heart wi terror numb.
Whan I mind on dat nicht, yet, I could – yis – I could go an skelp her bum.

At dat time, I'd a bune tree or fower year auld, sho a lass in her teens.
Sho micht a hed mair sense, I'm sure, as tae fill me wi nightmare draems.
An da idder eens aa got a keeck at seein me sae fairt.
Wanse hit cam dark, I did me best ta hadd clear o da stairs.

Bit dere cam a nicht I ventured up fir a book I'd left i da room.
A fire wis on, so da gluid fae dat kinda brichtened up da gloom;
I spanged up trow, as quick as I could (me heart wis baetin fast),
I skreiched an ran, never lookin back, till I gained da door, at last.

Bit as I guid ta come doon agen, me heart stuid still wi faer,
Fir whit sees I bit yon twa green een, glowerin at me dere …
I gae a yell an ran back in, an jamp apo a chair.
Ta win doonstairs, past dat twa een, wis mair as I could dare.

Whin da fire lowed doon da room grew dark, so hit wis edder do or die.
So I gaddered aa da strent I hed, med up me mind ta try.
I yelled agen, an med a dive, never lookin whar I guid.
I took da stairs in twa big jumps, an sae gained da idder side.

Poor cat! I winder whit sho tocht hed ten a haud o me.
Nae faer sho'd led her at ta sleep, an draem aboot da spree
Dat sho wid hae whan folk wir in bed, an aa da hoose wis still.
Dan oot sho'd go, meet in wi 'Tom' wha hunted ower da hill.

Whan late at nicht I guid ta bed, da blankets ower me head,
Hit cam dat haet I couldna braethe, bit look oot I never could.
Fir faer o rats an mice an men an Heavens kens whit else
Dat I aye tocht wir sittin dere, ready ta jimp fae aff da shelf.

Ootside da bedroom doors twa barrels stuid – een fir aetmel, een fir flooer.
(Whan dey wir filled, I'm tellin you, dere wis a boannie stoor.)
On da wan neist my room door, da shoppin basket stuid.
(Every week some een guid tae da shop, an filled him richt tae da lid.)

Athin his boddam, alang da saems, some crumbs wir sure ta be,
A fine huntin grund fir peerie mice whin dey guid on da spree.
So ee nicht I hears dis scrufflin soond … (I'd surely stuckin oot me lug).
I gae a yell, banged on da waa, an roared an near waakened aa da dead.

"Come up at wanse, an kyill dat moose! I canna win tae sleep!"
Yet aa da time, I tell it noo, I wis near aboot tae greet.
On tinkin back, whit a fuil wis I, faert fir a peerie moose,
Bit at yon time, my heart stuid still, an I waakened aa da hoose.

Dis faers I hed wir fostered tu. Wir folk dey hed nae tocht
Fir whan I ran an skreiched wi faer, dey juist aa sat back an laached.
"He surely hed a hadd o dee yon time," me aunt, sho used ta joke.
Bit hit worried me ta tink dat I wisna brave, laek idder folk.

In days geen by, whin I wis young, bathrooms dey wir none.
So whan we needed ta spend a penny, ootside we hed ta run.
I never ken whit wye hit wis dat I couldna a hed aa dun wi daylicht
Bit I surely wis ower lazy dan, fir hit wis aye pittin aaf fir nicht.

Sometimes da mon – Guid bless her still – wid lichten up my gaet.
Bit idder nichts I mind wis dark, wi rain or wind or sleet.
Bit oot be nort I hed ta go, da stars me only guide,
Tho sister Meg sho aye cam wi me, an sho never left me side.

Be nort da byre dere wis a burn, crossed be a muckle brig;
Dat wis my bathroom – believe it or no, bit you can tak my wird.
Da watter guldered doon da steep on it's wye tawards da sea,
An sae keepit aa thing pritty an clean, which wis juist as weel fir me.

I mind ae nicht I'd backit me kert ower far ower da rim
I lost me fittin, ower I guid, fairly tumpit in.
Meg, sho heard a skreich an splash, an roared: "Whit's happened dee?"
Weel micht sho aks, whin dere wis I, as weet as I could be.

Anidder night, at naiter's caal, we baith hed ventured furt.
On comin back, "him" hard on me heels, I lost me smuck ida purt.
Bit on I ran, an skreiched wi faer, laevin Maggie ida rear.
Heth if "he" catched her da sorrow care, sae lang as I wan clear.

Whin I wis mebbe echt or nine year auld, dan we got an ootside lavatree,
Bit still an on, dat med nae odds tae dis faer dat hed a haud o me.
On darksome nichts I'd look at Meg wi mony a wink an nod,
Sho'd lay by her sock an oot sho'd come, my ever faithful guide.

Fir ta geng intae dat peerie oot-hoose mesel! Dat faer gae me da creeps,
Fir if I met "him", as sure as fate he'd hed me dere fir keeps.
An fir aa I kent, I micht even a fun "him" sittin on da saet,
An just ta tochts o dat green een could fairly lowse da swaet.

Bit, at last, dis bairnly faers dey passed (as aa things pass in life).
Hit widna a lookit aafil weel, ta hae been a faertie wife –
Bit I still mind an winder yit, whedder bairns noo are as fairt,
As I mind back foo scared I wis o aa things intae da dark.

Wi switches here an switches dere I widna tink dey'll be,
Fir dey're never bun exposed tae da dark, as da laeks o dee an me.
We mind da times we med wir wye, wi mony a grope an grovel,
An fan maistly aa dat we lookit for be usin da feel o wir trivel.

Noo, aa you folk wi peerie bairns, an der naitril faer i da dark,
Never ever bend you doon tae der lug tae gie a hark.
Fir I canna forgyit dat feelin yit – dat risin o da hair
An da faer I felt whan I cam in mind o dat twa een on da stair.

Auld age brings faers, I'm heard dem say (an I ken dat tae be true),
I hoop I dunna live ta see dat time – I don't mind tellin you,
Fir if I geng trow yon agen, I'll jump richt oot o me sark.
Bit, nae faer, hit'll be somethin idder dan – an no twa cat's een i da dark!

Chrissie Sandison
22nd December, 1970
Published in *Shetland Life*, issue 14

Da Tap O Mitchell's Hill

Dere's a special place at Clousta
(My tochts aft stray dere still)
Some day shune I'll mak my wye
An clim up Mitchell's Hill.
Nae maiter whit ert da wind is at
Some shelter I will fin
Dere's muckle runnies stickin up
On which my back I'll lin …
Or I'll streetch oot, flat apon me back
An gaze up at da sky.
Aal aertly cares I'll cast aside
As dere, content, I'll lie.
I'll mebbe hae a peerie sleep,
Da sunsheen on my face,
Dan up I'll staand an look aboot
Dat bonnie paecefil place.
Da view wan gyits fae up sae high
Can tak wan's braeth awa!
I aften see it intae my mind
It's never dat far awaa …
Stenness seems dat near at haund
An aa da headlaands in atween
I'll aesy reck across Noonsbrough
An shak haunds wi "Da Teef o da Nean".
On Mitchell's Hill, da grund is hard
Or I'd geng an mak me will
An aks fir tae be laid tae rest
On da tap o Mitchell's Hill.
I dunna ken wha Mitchell wis

Nor whaar in Clousta he did dwell,
He cood ha been a witless sowl,
Da sam as I am, mesel.

Chrissie Sandison
Published in *Shetland Life*, issue 30

Glossary

Aa – all
Aabody – everybody
Aafil head o' hair – a shock of hair
Abune – above
Aff – off
Aye – always

Baand – band
Bairn – child
Banks – sea cliffs
Be wast da hoose – to the west of the house
Ben; ben-end – the best room
Ben da hoose – in the best room
Benkled – dented
Bing – heap
Blaand – whey
Blinky – torch
Blyde – glad
Boddy – person
Braand iron – gridiron
Brönnie – thick scone
Broo – brow of a hill
Brooks – heaps/piles
Brugs – mounds
Bucksed – trudged heavily
Buggie-flay – to skin a sheep
But; but-end – the living-room
By – past

Caa; caain – to drive (sheep etc); driving/gathering sheep
Cliv – hoof; trotter

Clockin hen – broody hen
Clod – small, hard peat
Come wi da sea – washed ashore
Cowld – cold
Craa-head – chimney head
Crappen – fish livers mixed with flour, seasoning and (sometimes) cooked in
    a large fish head
Crö – sheep pen
Cuttin girse – the cut grass/hay

Da – the
Daek – wall (faely daek – wall made of turf)
Daffik – wooden bucket
Dan – then
De – you
Dellin – digging
Dey – they
Dicht – to wipe, to clean
Didna – didn't
Dir – their
Docken – the common dock (plant)
Doon – down
Doosed – thudded
Dreep – drip
Drookled – soaked
Du – you
Dubb – bog; muddy pool
Dugs – dogs
Dukes – ducks
Du'll – you will
Dunderin – thundering noise
Dunna – don't
Dy – your

Ebb – shoreline exposed at ebb tide
Edder – other

Ee – one; eye
Een – one; eyes
Efter – after
Efter stammerin – a transom in the stern of a boat
Ert – direction
Essy kert – refuse vehicle

Face o' da banks – side of the sea-cliffs
Fae – from
Fairt – afraid
Firsmo – snubbing; a rebuke etc.
(Having a) fit o' da snippers – to sulk, dort
Flaas – heather turfs torn by hand; turfs cut from top of peat bank before
    peat cutting
Flytin – scolding
Fok – folk

Gaad – exclamation of disgust (eg. taste, smell)
Gaet – pathway
Geng – go
Girns – snarls, growls
Girse – grass
Gluff; gluffed-laek – fright; apprehensive, scared looking
Goon – gown
Goonie – nightdress
Gowled – cried loudly, sobbed
Grow – grow
Guizer – person in disguise

Hairst – autumn; the harvest
Hamely – homely
Hap – shawl
Hed – had
Heth – a mild oath
Hochs – thighs

I – in
Ida – in the
Ir – are

Jimp – jump
Johnnie Walker – whisky
Joost – just
Jumble-kirn – a churn
Jüst – just

Kale – cabbage
Ken – know
Kent – knew; known
Kerryin – carrying
Kishie – straw basket
Klett – a rock on the seashore
Klik – boyfriend
Kye – cattle
Kyist – chest

Laachter – laughter
Laar – gentle breeze
Laek – like
Lang – long
Lass – girl
Lirks – creases
Lowin' – aflame, burning
Lum – chimney

Möld – earth, soil
Mön – moon
Moorie caavie - blizzard
Moorie faels – turfs
Muckle – large

Nae – no, none
Needna – needn't

Neeps – turnips
Noo – now
Noost – a place, usually near a beach or shore, where a boat is drawn up
Nuggin – nudging or rocking with the foot

Oiler – a drain (in a byre)
Onkerry – a carry-on, disturbance
Oo – wool
Oot – out
Ower – over
Ower-blyde – very glad

Paet – peat
Paet-reek – smoke from burning peat
Peenie(s) – apron(s)
Peerie – small
Peester – squeal or squeak
Piltik waand – fishing rod
Pones (poans) – turfs (thinly cut)
Pooskin – poking

Raans – fish roe
Redd oot – sort out
Restin chair – wooden seat with back and arms
Rodd – road
Roddy-men – road workers
Ruif – roof

Sae – so
Saut – salt
Sembled tagedder – stuck or joined together
Set tü – fight, argument
Shilk – chew
Sho – she
Shun – small loch

Shuttin – shooting
Sitten (eggs) – partly incubated
Sic – such
Sillock – young coalfish
Skite – peek, look
Skule – school
Skyumpie – large mossy peat
Smisslens – sand-gaper shellfish
Snaa – snow
Sniffin da cork – having a drink (of alcohol)
Sock – a piece of knitting
Spoots – razor-clam
Stamick – stomach
Swaarloch – a boggy, miry hole
Swab – cloth
Sweein – stinging, tingling

Ta – to
Taen aff – slaughtered
Taen da saut – salted (fish or meat)
Taft – a thwart in a boat
Tak – take
Tang – seaweed
Tatties – potatoes
Tattit rug – rug made of thick worsted yarn
Tocht – thought
Tooms – thumbs
Toon – the enclosed arable land of a croft or farm
Trachle – wearisome work
Trampit – trampled
Trang kempin – busy competing with each other
Trowie tings – troll-like children
Trukkit gaet – trampled path
Twa – two
Twa geng o' spades – team of workers (digging a field)

Twafauld – doubled up, bent over
Twartbacks – tie beam between rafters
Twartree – two or three, a few

Uptak – responsibility

Vergin – working (messy)
Voar – spring time

Waar; waarblades – seaweed
Wan – one
Wanse – once
Wha – who
Whaar – where
Whin – when
Wid – would
Widda – would have
Widna – wouldn't
Winder – wonder
Wir – our
Wirset – wool, worsted
Wirt – worth
Wis – us
Wye – way

Yalkin – yelping, barking
Yoag – large horse-mussel